World Economic and Financia

FISCAL MONITOR
April 2011

Shifting Gears
Tackling Challenges
on the Road to Fiscal Adjustment

International Monetary Fund

©2011 International Monetary Fund
Second printing (revised), April 2011

Production: IMF Multimedia Services Division
Typesetting: Maria Delariarte and Nadia Malikyar

Cataloging-in-Publication Data

Fiscal monitor—Washington, D.C. : International Monetary Fund, 2009–
        v. ;   cm. — (World economic and financial surveys, 0258-7440)

        Twice a year.
        Some issues have also thematic titles.

        1. Finance, Public—Periodicals. 2. Finance, Public—Forecasting—Periodicals. 3. Fiscal
policy—Periodicals. 4. Fiscal policy—Forecasting—Periodicals. 5. Financial crises—Periodicals.
6. Global Financial Crisis, 2008–2009—Periodicals. I. International Monetary Fund. II. Series: World
economic and financial surveys.
HJ101.F57

Please send orders to:
International Monetary Fund, Publication Services
P.O. Box 92780, Washington, D.C. 20090, U.S.A.
Telephone: (202) 623-7430   Fax: (202) 623-7201
E-mail: publications@imf.org
Internet: www.imfbookstore.org

Contents

Tables

Statistical Tables

Preface

The projections included in this *Fiscal Monitor* are based on the same database used for the April 2011 *World Economic Outlook* (WEO) and *Global Financial Stability Report* (GFSR) (and are referred to as "IMF staff projections"). The fiscal projections refer to the general government unless otherwise indicated. Short-term fiscal projections are based on officially announced budgets, adjusted for differences between the national authorities and the IMF staff regarding macroeconomic assumptions. The medium-term fiscal projections incorporate policy measures that are judged by the IMF staff as likely to be implemented. For countries supported by an IMF arrangement, the medium-term projections are those under the arrangement. In cases where the IMF staff has insufficient information to assess the authorities' budget intentions and prospects for policy implementation, an unchanged cyclically adjusted primary balance is assumed, unless indicated otherwise. Country-specific assumptions are detailed in the Methodological and Statistical Appendix, which precedes the Statistical Tables. This issue of the *Fiscal Monitor* includes a new table (Statistical Table 9) on structural fiscal indicators.

The *Fiscal Monitor* is prepared by the IMF Fiscal Affairs Department under the supervision of Carlo Cottarelli, Director of the Department, and Philip Gerson, Senior Advisor. This issue is coordinated by Manmohan S. Kumar and Paolo Mauro. Principal contributors include Giovanni Callegari, Timothy Irwin, Laura Jaramillo Mayor, Jiri Jonas, Michael Keen, Andrea Lemgruber, Marialuz Moreno-Badia, Andrea Schaechter, Mauricio Soto, Anita Tuladhar, and Mauricio Villafuerte. Matias Antonio, Petra Dacheva, Raquel Gomez Sirera, and Julia Guerreiro provided research assistance. In addition, contributions were provided by Emre Alper, Jochen Andritzky, Emanuele Baldacci, Xavier Debrun, Julio Escolano, Marc Gerard, Bertrand Gruss, Jimmy McHugh, Iva Petrova, Anna Shabunina, and Jaejoon Woo.

Maria Delariarte and Nadia Malikyar provided excellent administrative and editorial assistance. From the IMF External Relations Department, Nancy Morrison edited the volume, and Sean Culhane and Michael Harrup managed its production.

The analysis has benefited from comments and suggestions by staff from other IMF departments. Both projections and policy considerations are those of the IMF staff and should not be attributed to Executive Directors or to their national authorities.

This version of the Fiscal Monitor is available in full on the IMF's website, www.imf.org.

Further inquiries may be sent to the Fiscal Policy and Surveillance Division, Fiscal Affairs Department.

International Monetary Fund
700 19th Street, N.W.
Washington, D.C. 20431, U.S.A.
www.imf.org/
Fax: (202) 623-6343

Main Themes

Fiscal sustainability risks remain elevated, as progress in some regions has been offset by delays in fiscal consolidation in others. Most advanced economies are reducing fiscal deficits this year, but the United States has put adjustment on hold, and fiscal adjustment had been postponed in Japan relative to the pace envisaged in the November Fiscal Monitor, *even before the recent earthquake, which will involve additional fiscal costs. Debt ratios are still rising in most advanced economies, and financing needs are at historical highs. Although market conditions are now favorable for most, markets have in the past reacted late and abruptly to deteriorating fiscal conditions. The fiscal outlook for emerging economies is more favorable, but this reflects in part the tailwinds of high asset and commodity prices, low interest rates, and strong capital inflows; their reversal could leave fiscal positions exposed in many cases. Moreover, some of these economies may be gradually overheating. For advanced economies, steady annual progress, starting now, toward bringing debt ratios to prudent levels in the medium term is essential. Emerging economies should use revenues associated with current favorable conditions to rebuild fiscal space rather than to increase spending in the near term. Both groups should make progress on structural reforms to enhance growth and equity, and strengthen fiscal institutions and transparency.*

Headline deficits in advanced economies fell in 2010, but this reflected the economic recovery and declining needs to support the financial sector rather than tighter policies. By contrast, most advanced economies do plan to tighten fiscal policy this year. Nevertheless, deficits will remain large, the average general government gross debt ratio is projected to breach the 100 percent threshold for the first time since the aftermath of World War II, and gross financing needs will reach record levels. Moreover, the United States has deferred consolidation plans for this year, introducing further stimulus. Prior to the earthquake that struck the country on March 11, Japan's fiscal stance was broadly neutral, with a postponement of fiscal adjustment relative to the pace envisaged in the November *Fiscal Monitor*. The earthquake will now inevitably involve significant additional fiscal costs, the magnitude of which cannot be properly estimated at this early stage.

The United States needs to accelerate the adoption of credible measures to reduce debt ratios. In Japan, when estimates of the overall fiscal cost of disaster relief and reconstruction become available, it will be necessary to incorporate them into plans for steady medium-term fiscal adjustment, backed up by measures more clearly identified than in the past. In the euro area, where fiscal consolidation has largely unfolded according to plans, progress in identifying a comprehensive pan-European approach to crisis management is welcome, but important details remain to be agreed. In all advanced economies, if growth this year proves faster than in the baseline scenario presented in the April 2011 *World Economic Outlook* (WEO), additional revenues should be saved; in the event of a slowdown, countries with fiscal space should allow the automatic stabilizers to operate. For most advanced economies, medium- and long-term spending pressures for pensions and especially health care remain to be addressed.

Deficits in emerging economies fell last year and will do so again this year—even after discounting for faster growth. In the face of rising inflationary pressures, some emerging economies are taking appropriate advantage of supportive macroeconomic conditions to achieve significant improvements in their cyclically adjusted primary balances. Others need to do more. Emerging economies need to resist the temptation in the near term to use current favorable tailwinds to boost spending and instead should rebuild fiscal buffers.

Following a large countercyclical stimulus in 2009, low-income economies tightened fiscal policy significantly last year and will tighten again this year, though more modestly, making good progress in rebuilding buffers drawn on in response to the crisis. Going forward, they need to balance critical spending needs—including those to address the social costs of high commodity prices—with fiscal sustainability concerns.

Across income levels, fiscal institutions need to be strengthened, including those aimed at improving fiscal transparency, to help ensure that fiscal targets are credibly achieved. There is evidence that faced with increasing fiscal pressures, some countries are resorting to accounting stratagems to meet their fiscal targets.

In all countries where deficit reduction is required to restore debt ratios to prudent levels, action is needed to ensure that the burdens of adjustment and benefits of economic recovery are distributed equitably. This is a key condition to make the adjustment sustainable.

Fiscal Deficits and Debts: Developments and Outlook

At a Glance

Fiscal deficits started to decline across all income groups in 2010, although mostly as a result of the improved macroeconomic environment. In 2011, fiscal plans are diverging significantly across advanced economies, partly reflecting differences in intensity of market pressure. Over the medium term, consolidation efforts on current policies will wind down, leaving headline and cyclically adjusted deficits in excess of precrisis levels. Countries delaying adjustment in 2011 will face more significant challenges to meet their medium-term objectives. Over the remainder of the decade, substantial further adjustment will be required to eventually restore debt ratios to prudent levels, especially in advanced economies. The challenge is even greater when the impact of trends affecting entitlement spending is taken into account. Indeed, rising spending on health care is the main risk to fiscal sustainability, with an impact on long-run debt ratios that, absent reforms, will dwarf that of the financial crisis.

Developments in 2010 and Projections for 2011

As most advanced economies shift to fiscal tightening this year, the largest ones lag

Fiscal policy continued to support economic activity in 2010. The average headline deficit in *advanced economies* was 7¾ percent of GDP, about

1 percentage point lower than in 2009 (Table 1.1).[1] However, this decline reflects the reduced need for government support to the financial sector in the United States, and stronger than expected growth.[2] Indeed, headline fiscal balances in almost all advanced economies were better than projected in the November 2010 *Fiscal Monitor*, thanks largely to some recovery in cyclical revenues and lower-than-projected spending (especially in Italy and Spain). In cyclically adjusted terms, however, the average deficit increased by ¼ percent of potential GDP in 2010, as implementation of stimulus measures peaked.

Striking differences are emerging in how fiscal policy will be managed across advanced economies in 2011. The degree of tightening appears to be correlated with the extent of market pressure, as countries facing higher market interest rates are generally reducing their deficits faster (Figure 1.1).

- In the *United States*, fiscal adjustment is being delayed. The stimulus package adopted in December 2010 (consisting of the extension of tax cuts and emergency unemployment benefits—see the January 2011 *Fiscal Monitor* update for details) is projected to contribute to an increase in the general government deficit to 10¾ percent of GDP, the largest among advanced economies this year. The United States is the only large advanced economy (aside from Japan—see below) aiming at an increased cyclically adjusted deficit this year, despite a narrowing (although still large) output gap (Figure 1.2). While targeted measures to address the high social costs of still weak housing and labor markets could be justified, the composition of the stimulus package means that its growth

---

[1] All averages in this *Fiscal Monitor* are weighted by GDP in purchasing power parity terms, unless noted otherwise.

[2] In 2010, government support to the financial sector (recorded as part of the deficit in the United States) was approximately ¼ percent of GDP, 2¼ percent of GDP lower than in 2009. The share of the United States in total GDP for the advanced economies is almost 40 percent.

Table 1.1. Fiscal Balances, 2008–12

	2008	2009	2010	Projections		Difference from November 2010 *Fiscal Monitor*		
				2011	2012	2010	2011	2012
Overall Balance (Percent of GDP)								
World	-2.0	-6.7	-5.6	-4.7	-3.5	0.4	0.2	0.2
Advanced Economies	-3.6	-8.8	-7.7	-7.1	-5.2	0.5	-0.3	-0.1
United States	-6.5	-12.7	-10.6	-10.8	-7.5	0.5	-1.1	-0.9
Euro Area	-2.1	-6.4	-6.0	-4.4	-3.6	0.7	0.7	0.7
France[1]	-3.3	-7.5	-7.0	-5.8	-4.9	1.0	0.3	-0.1
Germany	0.1	-3.0	-3.3	-2.3	-1.5	1.2	1.4	1.4
Italy	-2.7	-5.3	-4.5	-4.3	-3.5	0.6	0.0	0.1
Spain	-4.2	-11.1	-9.2	-6.2	-5.6	0.0	0.7	0.7
Japan	-4.2	-10.3	-9.5	-10.0	-8.4	0.1	-1.1	-0.3
United Kingdom	-4.9	-10.3	-10.4	-8.6	-6.9	-0.3	-0.5	-0.6
Canada	0.1	-5.5	-5.5	-4.6	-2.8	-0.6	-1.6	-0.6
Others	2.0	-1.0	0.2	0.9	1.6	0.9	0.8	0.7
Emerging Economies	-0.6	-4.9	-3.8	-2.6	-2.2	0.4	0.7	0.6
Asia	-2.4	-4.7	-4.2	-3.4	-2.7	0.4	0.5	0.5
China	-0.4	-3.1	-2.6	-1.6	-0.9	0.3	0.4	0.3
India	-8.0	-10.0	-9.4	-8.3	-7.5	0.2	0.5	0.9
ASEAN-5	-0.8	-3.7	-2.7	-2.8	-2.4	0.3	0.1	0.1
Europe	0.6	-6.2	-4.4	-2.3	-2.3	0.7	1.7	1.0
Russia	4.9	-6.3	-3.6	-1.6	-1.7	1.2	2.0	1.2
Latin America	-0.7	-3.7	-2.9	-2.2	-2.2	-0.3	0.0	0.0
Brazil	-1.4	-3.1	-2.9	-2.4	-2.6	-1.2	-1.2	-0.9
Mexico	-1.3	-4.8	-4.1	-1.8	-2.4	-0.5	1.3	0.3
Middle East and North Africa	-0.1	-2.9	-2.1	-4.9	-4.2	1.4	-1.4	-1.2
Low-Income Economies	-1.4	-4.2	-2.9	-2.6	-2.4	0.2	0.4	0.0
Oil Producers	4.7	-4.4	-1.4	1.2	1.3	1.8	3.4	2.3
G-20 Economies	-2.6	-7.5	-6.3	-5.7	-4.3	0.5	-0.1	0.0
Advanced G-20 Economies	-4.2	-9.4	-8.2	-8.0	-5.8	0.5	-0.6	-0.4
Emerging G-20 Economies	-0.4	-4.8	-3.6	-2.5	-2.1	0.4	0.6	0.6
Cyclically Adjusted Balance (Percent of Potential GDP)								
Advanced Economies	-3.3	-5.5	-5.7	-5.5	-4.2	0.4	-0.4	-0.2
United States[2]	-4.6	-6.8	-7.5	-8.1	-5.7	0.4	-1.0	-0.8
Euro Area	-2.9	-4.6	-4.2	-3.3	-2.8	0.7	0.6	0.6
France	-3.2	-5.5	-5.3	-4.3	-3.7	1.0	0.3	0.0
Germany	-1.0	-1.1	-2.4	-2.1	-1.5	0.9	0.8	1.0
Italy	-2.4	-3.2	-2.8	-2.7	-2.2	0.7	0.2	0.4
Spain	-5.3	-9.7	-7.5	-4.7	-4.6	0.0	0.7	0.7
Japan	-3.6	-7.0	-7.5	-8.3	-7.4	0.0	-1.1	-0.5
United Kingdom	-5.9	-8.5	-8.3	-6.6	-5.1	-0.3	-0.4	-0.4
Canada	0.0	-3.2	-4.0	-3.6	-2.2	-0.6	-1.6	-0.6
Others	0.5	-1.5	-0.8	-0.3	0.3	0.5	0.6	0.4
Emerging Economies	-2.4	-4.6	-4.1	-3.2	-2.7	-0.1	0.0	-0.1
Asia	-3.2	-5.2	-4.5	-3.6	-2.8	-0.2	-0.1	-0.2
China	-0.9	-3.4	-2.9	-1.8	-1.1	0.3	0.4	0.5
India	-10.2	-11.0	-10.0	-8.8	-7.7	-1.3	-1.6	-2.0
ASEAN-5	-1.5	-2.8	-2.0	-2.6	-2.2	1.3	0.5	0.1
Europe	-0.4	-4.1	-3.2	-2.2	-2.2	0.5	1.0	0.8
Russia	3.5	-3.5	-1.8	-0.6	-1.3	1.1	1.8	1.0
Latin America	-1.4	-2.9	-3.1	-2.5	-2.7	-0.6	-0.3	-0.6
Brazil	-2.1	-2.0	-3.0	-2.5	-2.6	-1.2	-1.3	-0.9
Mexico	-1.8	-4.4	-4.1	-2.1	-2.7	-1.4	0.2	-0.6
G-20 Economies	-3.0	-5.2	-5.2	-4.9	-3.8	0.2	-0.3	-0.3
Advanced G-20 Economies	-3.4	-5.6	-6.0	-6.1	-4.5	0.4	-0.6	-0.3
Emerging G-20 Economies	-2.3	-4.6	-4.0	-3.1	-2.7	-0.1	0.0	-0.2
Memorandum Items:								
Overall Balance								
Advanced Economies[2]	-3.3	-7.8	-7.6	-7.1	-5.2	0.3	-0.3	-0.1
United States[2]	-5.7	-10.2	-10.4	-10.7	-7.4	0.3	-1.1	-0.9

Sources: IMF staff estimates and projections.

Note: All country averages are PPP-GDP weighted using 2009 weights. Projections are based on staff assessment of current policies. The sample of emerging economies has been extended compared with the November 2010 *Fiscal Monitor*. (See "Fiscal Policy Assumptions" in the Methodological and Statistical Appendix.)

[1] For 2010, based on authorities' data as of March 31, 2011 (not yet reflected in the April 2011 WEO).

[2] Excluding financial sector support recorded above the line.

Figure 1.1. Advanced Economies: Change in Cyclically Adjusted Primary Balances, 2010–11, and Government Bond Yields, 2010

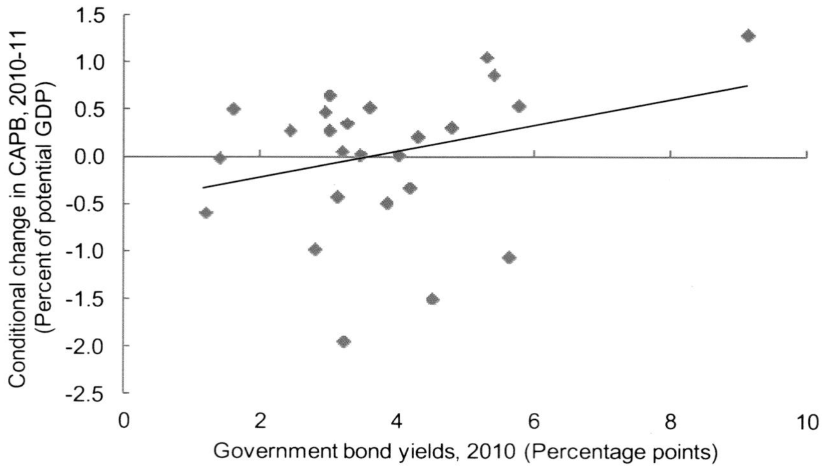

Sources: Datastream; and IMF staff estimates and projections.
Note: The vertical axis reports the residuals from a regression for a sample of 26 advanced economies of the change in the cyclically adjusted primary balance (CAPB) between 2010 and 2011 on the level of the CAPB in 2010, the change in the CAPB between 2007 and 2010, the unemployment rate in 2010, and the increase in the unemployment rate between 2007 and 2010.

impact will be small relative to its fiscal costs (April 2011 WEO). The deficit would be lower if the federal government were compelled to adhere to the current Continuing Resolution for a significant portion of the rest of FY2011.[3]

- In *Japan*, the fiscal stance was expected to be broadly neutral prior to the earthquake, as the expiration of earlier stimulus measures was being offset by increases in transfers. In the aftermath of the earthquake, the government is now expected to adopt a supplementary budget to support the relief efforts, including by tapping the available cash reserves (approximately 0.3 percent of GDP). Discussions are ongoing on how to finance the support package, with alternatives ranging from issuance of new bonds to a temporary tax hike.

---

[3] More generally, the U.S. fiscal stance remains highly uncertain given the ongoing discussions in Congress about this year's federal spending levels.

Figure 1.2. Advanced Economies: Change in Cyclically Adjusted Balance and Change in Output Gap, 2011

(Percent of potential GDP)

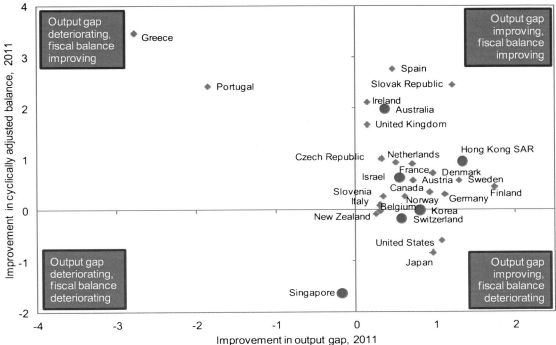

Sources: IMF staff estimates and projections.
Note: The output gap is defined as the difference between actual and potential GDP. If the output gap is deteriorating, there is greater spare capacity in the economy. Circles denote countries with output levels above potential in 2011. For Norway, data refer to cyclically adjusted non-oil balance.

- In contrast, *Europe* is tightening. The overall deficit in the *euro area* is expected to fall sharply, due to withdrawal of stimulus and the lower impact of automatic stabilizers. Tax base widening (Germany), wage bill freezes (Italy), pension reform (France and Spain), and expenditure cuts and a value-added tax (VAT) rate hike (Spain) will also contribute. Greece, Ireland, and Portugal have adopted further consolidation measures to enhance the credibility of their front-loaded plans. In the *United Kingdom*, cuts in real discretionary spending and a VAT rate increase will be the primary factors behind a projected decline in the cyclically adjusted deficit of 1¾ percent of GDP, the largest adjustment among major advanced economies.

- In some *other advanced economies*, the consolidation continues, facilitated by the strong pickup in economic activity, with output projected close to or above potential in Australia and Korea. In these countries, buoyant cyclical revenues, complete withdrawal of the fiscal stimulus, and expenditure restraint are leading both headline and cyclically adjusted balances to improve. On the other hand, the recent earthquake in New Zealand will have a significant impact on the fiscal balance this year.

Slippages are emerging in some economies with respect to what was envisaged in medium-term fiscal adjustment plans (Table 1.2). Shortfalls reflect new stimulus measures (United States), more pessimistic macroeconomic projections in this *Fiscal Monitor* (Canada and Portugal), natural disasters (Japan), and a worsened outlook for subnational governments (Canada). In contrast, Germany is expected to overperform, owing to stronger growth. Projected adjustment is close to plans in many EU advanced economies. In some cases, revisions have affected the composition of adjustment (United Kingdom). Altogether, the average deficit for advanced economies is expected to fall by ¾ percent of GDP to 7 percent. In cyclically adjusted terms, the improvement amounts to ¼ percent of GDP, far less than projected in the November 2010 *Fiscal Monitor*.

Deficits remain well above the levels that would stabilize debt ratios. Gross general government debt ratios rose in almost all advanced economies in 2010 (except in Estonia, Israel, Korea, Singapore, Sweden, and Switzerland). The increase was 6½ percentage points of GDP in Germany, owing to financial support operations (Box 1.1). Among smaller countries, the largest increases were observed in Greece and Ireland, the increase in the latter also reflecting financial sector support operations. While nearly all advanced economies will narrow their deficits in 2011 (with the largest reductions in the Slovak Republic and Spain), two-thirds will record further increases in debt (Figure 1.3), with the average breaching the 100-percent-of-GDP threshold.

Table 1.2. Fiscal Balances in 2011: Medium-Term Plans and IMF Staff Projections

(Percent of each projection's GDP)

	Medium-Term Plans	*Fiscal Monitor* Projections	Difference
Australia	-2.7	-2.5	0.2
Canada[1]	-2.7	-4.1	-1.4
France	-6.0	-5.8	0.2
Germany	-3.5	-2.3	1.2
Greece	-7.3	-7.4	-0.1
India[1]	-6.8	-8.1	-1.3
Ireland	-10.0	-10.8	-0.8
Italy	-4.0	-4.3	-0.3
Japan[2]	-8.0	-10.0	-2.0
Korea[3]	0.5	2.2	1.7
Latvia	-5.3	-5.3	0.0
Lithuania	-5.8	-6.0	-0.2
Mexico	-2.3	-1.8	0.5
Portugal[4]	-4.6	-5.6	-1.0
Russian Federation[1]	-3.7	-1.6	2.1
South Africa[1]	-5.3	-5.5	-0.2
Spain	-6.0	-6.2	-0.2
Turkey	-4.4	-1.7	2.7
United Kingdom[1]	-7.5	-8.1	-0.6
United States[1]	-9.2	-10.5	-1.3

Sources: Country authorities' data and IMF staff projections; averages weighted by GDP at PPP.

Note: The table compares the 2011 fiscal balances envisaged under the medium-term adjustment plans announced during the first eight months of 2010 (and described in Bornhorst and others, 2010) and the current IMF staff projections for the 2011 fiscal balances.

[1] Fiscal year projections: April 2011–March 2012 in Canada, India, and the United Kingdom; October 2010–September 2011 in the United States; April 2011–March 2012 in South Africa. Data refer to the federal government for the Russian Federation and the United States, and to the public sector for the United Kingdom.

[2] Authorities' projections converted from fiscal to calendar year. Projections include disaster-related spending of 0.8 percent of GDP. A difference of 1.1 percent of GDP already existed in the November 2010 *Fiscal Monitor* projections.

[3] Refers to central government only.

[4] The IMF staff projections differ from the authorities' largely because they are based on less optimistic macroeconomic projections. The projections were prepared prior to the authorities' request for financial assistance.

Box 1.1. Financial Sector Support and Recovery to Date

Despite better overall conditions, some sizable financial sector support measures have been enacted recently. Significant outlays occurred in *Germany* (preliminarily estimated at 7 percent of GDP), reflecting an asset transfer from Hypo Real Estate to FSM Wertmanagement (the German Asset Management Agency). In the *United Kingdom*, new outlays are related to additional financial support for Northern Rock (½ percent of GDP). In *Ireland*, bank recapitalization costs amounted to 30 percent of GDP (one-third of this has taken the form of investments by the National Pension Reserve Fund and hence does not increase general government debt). In addition, the National Asset Management Agency has issued government-guaranteed bonds equivalent to 19¼ percent of GDP for the purchase of bad assets. In *Spain*, the government injected capital amounting to 1.1 percent of GDP into the banking system via its bank support vehicle (FROB). Moreover, the government has extended the guarantee scheme for credit institutions until June 2011: the unused amount is 10 percent of GDP.

For a sample of advanced economies where support has been significant, the cumulative net direct cost since the beginning of the crisis amounts to 4¾ of GDP (see table). Most measures have expired or were not as heavily used as originally expected. By end-December 2010, the cumulative recovery of outlays stood at 1½ percent of GDP; the recovery rate (as a share of direct support) was 25 percent. The bulk of the recovery to date comes from the United States, where recovery has been fast. (The U.S. Congressional Budget Office [2010] projects the net direct cost of financial support through the Troubled Asset Relief Program at less than ¼ percent of GDP.)

Selected Advanced Economies: Recovery of Outlays and Net Cost of Financial Sector Support
(Latest available date; percent of 2010 GDP unless otherwise indicated)[1]

	Direct Support	Recovery	Net Direct Cost
Belgium	4.3	0.2	4.1
Ireland [2]	30.0	1.3	28.7
Germany [3]	10.8	0.1	10.7
Greece	5.1	0.1	5.0
Netherlands	14.4	8.4	6.0
Spain	2.9	0.9	2.0
United Kingdom	7.1	1.1	6.0
United States	5.2	1.8	3.4
Average	6.4	1.6	4.8
In billions of U.S. dollars	1,528	379	1,149

Sources: Country authorities; and IMF staff estimates.

Note: Fiscal outlays of the central government. In addition, some countries may have supported financial institutions via fiscal outlays at the subnational level or through other public sector institutions. For example, in Germany, capital injections from the Laender and KfW (development bank) amount to 1.1 percent of GDP; in Belgium, financial sector support from regional government amount to 1.6 percent of GDP.

[1] Cumulative since the beginning of the crisis—latest available data, ranging between end-December 2010 and end-March 2011.

[2] Direct support does not include asset purchases by the National Asset Management Agency, as these are not financed directly through the general government but with government-guaranteed bonds.

[3] Direct support includes an estimated amount of €240 billion (9½ percent of GDP) for asset purchases.

Emerging economy deficits are falling, but are they doing so fast enough?

In 2010, deficits started declining in *emerging economies*, supported by sustained growth and, in some, higher commodity prices. The average general government deficit fell by 1 percent of GDP, with revenues surprising on the upside compared with the November 2010 *Fiscal Monitor*, in significant part owing to one-off or cyclical revenues (e.g., Brazil, India, and South Africa). Altogether, consolidation was much more contained (½ percent of GDP) in cyclically adjusted terms.

Consolidation is expected to accelerate in 2011. The average headline deficit is projected to fall by 1¼ percent of GDP (about 1 percent of GDP in cyclically adjusted terms). There are significant cross-country differences, though:

- Adjustment in *emerging Asia*, except for China and India, is limited. In India, however, the improvement in the headline balance falls short of initial plans and is broadly accounted for by continued strong revenues, restraint in wages, pensions, and interest, and improvements at the subnational level. In the ASEAN-5 (Indonesia, Malaysia, the Philippines, Singapore, and Thailand), the fiscal stance is broadly neutral, on average.

- Fiscal consolidation in *Latin America* is expected to continue in 2011. In Brazil, the government has announced a package of measures totaling about 1¼ percent of GDP to achieve its fiscal target (a primary surplus of about 3 percent of GDP). Policy lending to the national development bank (BNDES) is also projected to fall, after averaging 3 percent of GDP over the 2009–10 period. In Mexico, the fiscal balance is expected to improve, owing to higher oil prices and the continuing impact of tax increases introduced in 2010.

- Within *emerging Europe,* the improvement in the Russian Federation reflects a significant rise in oil and natural gas prices and discretionary consolidation measures. Stronger growth is likely to bring down Turkey's

Figure 1.3. Advanced Economies: Change in Overall Deficits and Gross General Government Debt, 2011

(Percent of GDP)

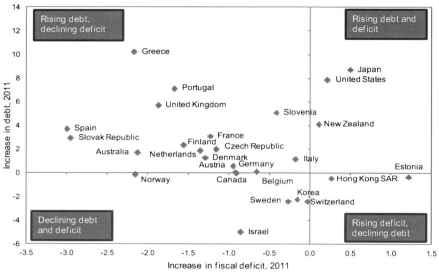

Source: IMF staff projections.
Note: Changes in debt and deficits refer to 2011 vis-à-vis 2010.

Figure 1.4. Emerging Economies: Change in Overall Deficits and Gross General Government Debt, 2011

(Percent of GDP)

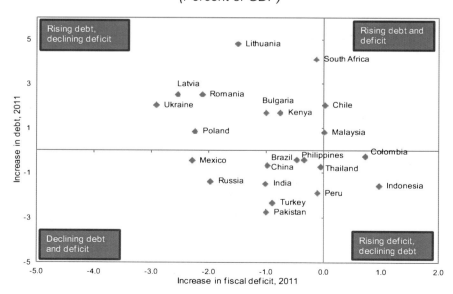

Source: IMF staff projections.
Note: Increases in debt and deficits are versus 2010.

Figure 1.5. Fiscal Balances in Oil-Producing Economies, Weighted Average
(Percent of GDP)

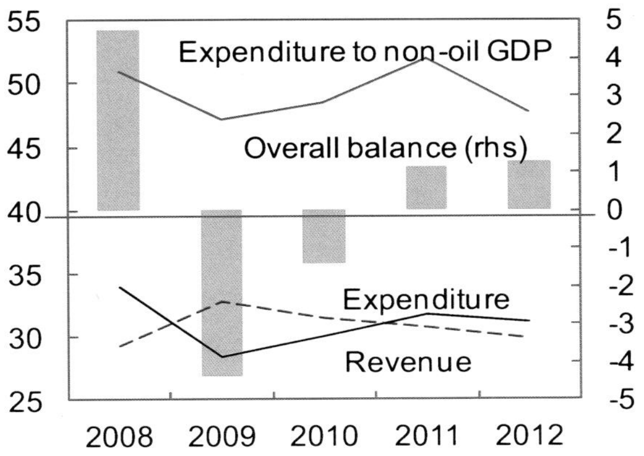

Source: IMF staff projections.

deficit faster than planned. Adjustment is significant in Bulgaria, Latvia, Lithuania, and Romania. In Hungary, the structural deficit (which excludes one-time increases in revenues) is expected to widen. In several economies, debt ratios will continue to rise, despite declining deficits (Figure 1.4).

- In the *Middle East* and *North Africa*, outcomes will hinge on policy responses to higher commodity prices and recent unrest in the region. Headline balances in oil-producing countries (in the region and elsewhere) are generally expected to improve (Figure 1.5). Deficits may widen in several oil importers, reflecting higher discretionary spending, particularly on subsidies to stabilize food and fuel prices and social transfers.

The pace of consolidation, however, seems to fall short of what would be warranted by cyclical developments. For many emerging economies, growth is buoyant, output is close to or above potential, and inflation is rising (April 2011 WEO). Nevertheless, cyclically adjusted primary balances are often projected to be substantially weaker than before the outset of the crisis (Figure 1.6). In some economies, fiscal policies continue to be expansionary even as GDP growth is on the upturn (Figure 1.7). Fiscal policy also appears insufficiently tight when viewed relative to a composite measure of the

Figure 1.6. Emerging Economies: Difference in Cyclically Adjusted Primary Balance, 2011, Compared with Precrisis Period

(Percent of potential GDP)

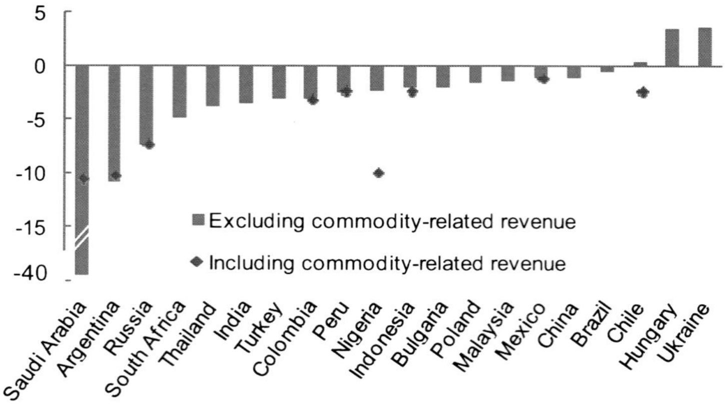

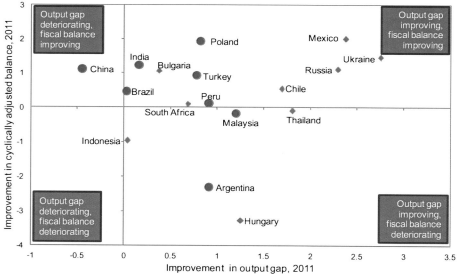

Sources: IMF staff estimates and projections.

Note: Precrisis deficits refer to 2004–07, subject to data availability. For Nigeria and Saudi Arabia, data reflect change in primary balance as percentage of non-oil GDP. For countries with significant commodity revenues (marked with red diamonds), changes in cyclically adjusted primary balances are shown both with and without these revenues.

Figure 1.7. Emerging Economies: Change in Cyclically Adjusted Balance and Change in Output Gap, 2011

(Percent of potential GDP)

Sources: IMF staff estimates and projections.

Note: The output gap is defined as the difference between actual and potential GDP. If the output gap is deteriorating, there is greater spare capacity in the economy. Circles denote countries with output level above potential in 2011. For Hungary, change in structural balance is reported.

Figure 1.8. Emerging Economies: Indicator of Cyclical Conditions and Fiscal Position

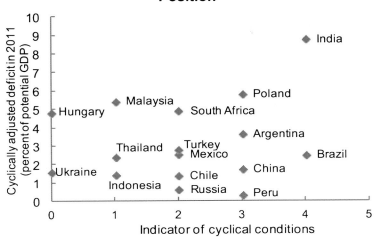

Sources: IMF staff estimates and projections.

Note: The indicator of cyclical conditions is a composite based upon the following variables: 2011–12 average inflation above 2009–10 average inflation; real economic growth above long-run average; output above potential; and positive net capital inflows. A subindicator for each of these variables is scored 1 if positive, 0 otherwise. The indicator is the sum of the subindicators of these variables. For Hungary and Mexico, the level of the structural deficit is reported.

cyclical position that includes not only the output gap but also the rate of output growth, expected inflation, and capital inflows. Based on this broader measure, Argentina, India, and Poland, in particular, are enjoying strong macroeconomic conditions while maintaining cyclically adjusted deficits exceeding 3 percent of GDP (Figure 1.8). This suggests that, in many countries, greater tightening would be appropriate.

Low-income economies are rebuilding buffers, but are also facing spending pressures

Following a large countercyclical stimulus in 2009, headline fiscal deficits in low-income countries improved strongly in 2010 (Table 1.3; Figure 1.9).[4] Revenues accounted for about two-thirds of the 1¼ percent of GDP improvement, reflecting the ongoing economic recovery and, for net

---

[4] The primary balance also improved by about 1 percentage point of GDP between 2009 and 2010. In view of data limitations and uncertainties regarding changes in potential growth in low-income economies, fiscal variables for this group are not adjusted for the cycle.

Table 1.3. Low-Income Economies: Fiscal Balances, 2008–12

(Percent of GDP)

	2008	2009	2010	Projections 2011	Projections 2012	Difference from November 2010 *Fiscal Monitor* 2010	Difference from November 2010 *Fiscal Monitor* 2011	Difference from November 2010 *Fiscal Monitor* 2012
Overall Balance								
Low-Income Economies	-1.4	-4.2	-2.9	-2.6	-2.4	0.2	0.4	0.0
Asia	-2.5	-5.7	-4.3	-3.6	-3.9	-0.6	-0.5	-1.0
Africa	-1.6	-2.9	-2.9	-2.5	-2.0	-0.5	0.3	-0.7
Latin America	0.7	-2.1	-0.1	-1.6	-1.1	2.8	0.9	1.4
Middle East, Eastern Europe, and Central Asia	1.0	-3.9	-0.8	-0.5	-0.2	2.2	2.4	2.6

Source: IMF staff projections.
Note: All country averages are PPP-GDP weighted using 2009 weights.

Figure 1.9. Overall Balance in Low-Income Economies

(Percent of GDP)

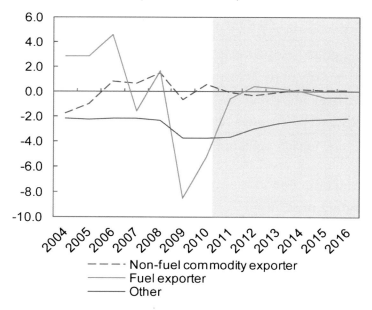

Source: IMF staff estimates.

exporters, rising commodity prices. For net commodity importers, revenues were also buoyant due to a sharp recovery in trade and associated gains in indirect taxes. On the spending side, past stimulus was mostly allowed to expire. New spending was contained, especially in regions with limited fiscal space in light of large increases in debt levels incurred during the crisis (Eastern Europe, Latin America, and the Middle East).

In 2011, the pace of fiscal consolidation is expected to slow, amid rising risks from food and fuel price increases. Headline deficits are projected to decline, on average, by ¼ percentage point of GDP. As a result of fuel price gains, sharper declines in deficits are expected among oil exporters (e.g., Chad). However, for fuel importers in particular, rising oil prices are likely to increase pressure for spending on wages and subsidies. Oil price increases since 2009 have been almost fully passed through to consumers in advanced economies, but only partially so in emerging and especially low-income economies (Box 1.2). The incomplete pass-through has led to lower tax revenues and higher subsidies, albeit with considerable variation across countries. On average, net gasoline taxes in 2010 are estimated to have declined by more than ¼ percent of GDP compared to 2009. While advanced economies saw an increase of ¼ percent of GDP, developing countries lost ½ percent of GDP in tax revenues. Revenue loss for diesel is likely to have been even higher. Likewise, rising food prices (which are now back at the peak levels attained during the food price spike of mid-2008) are damaging welfare and adding to fiscal challenges. The budgetary cost of greater food subsidies can be significant: the increase in subsidies was estimated at more than ½ percent of GDP during the 2007–08 spike in food prices, when many countries reduced taxes on food items (import duties and, to a lesser extent, VAT) or increased explicit subsidies (IMF, 2008). Recent political turmoil in the Middle East has led policymakers in many countries to consider additional social spending and public investment.

Box 1.2. Pass-Through and Fiscal Impact of Rising Fuel Prices

Pass-through of increases in international fuel prices to domestic prices has been limited in many countries in recent years (see tables and figure). In a sample of 93 countries, fewer than half fully passed through to domestic prices the run-up in world prices between end-2003 and mid-2008. Pass-through was highest for advanced European and oil-importing developing economies, and lowest in oil-exporting economies. Between mid-2008 and end-2008, despite the sharp drop in world prices, retail prices were held more stable, resulting in lower pass-through. Only nine countries (many in southeastern Europe and the Baltics) fully passed through the drop in world prices; 54 countries (developing and fuel-exporting emerging economies) passed through less than half the drop. From 2009 to end-2010, pass-through of rising international prices was once again partial, and generally lower than during the increase observed between 2003 and mid-2008, particularly for developing economies.

Pass-Through of Global Fuel Prices

	End-2003 to Mid-2008	Mid-2008 to End-2008	End-2008 to End-2010	Number of Countries
By Size of Pass-Through:		Number of countries		
> 1	44	9	38	...
Between .5 and 1	34	30	28	...
Between .25 and .5	7	21	9	...
< .25	8	33	18	...
		Median Pass-Through (ratio)		
By Economy:				
Advanced	1.02	0.57	0.98	31
Emerging	0.74	0.19	0.75	21
Developing	1.02	0.29	0.63	41
By Oil Trade:				
Exporter	0.55	0.02	0.75	19
Importer	1.02	0.48	0.81	74

Sources: IEA; GTZ; country authorities; Thompson Reuters; and IMF staff estimates.
Note: Pass-through is measured as the ratio of the change in domestic price index in local currency to the change in international spot price index, also measured in local currency, over the time horizon noted.

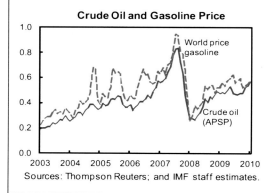

Crude Oil and Gasoline Price

World price gasoline

Crude oil (APSP)

Sources: Thompson Reuters; and IMF staff estimates.

Net Taxes
(US$ per liter)

	End-2003	Mid-2008	End-2008	End-2010	Number of Countries
By Economy:					
Advanced	0.65	0.86	1.02	0.97	31
Emerging	0.27	0.03	0.53	0.45	21
Developing	0.18	0.15	0.71	0.43	41
By Oil Trade:					
Exporter	0.36	-0.03	0.57	0.43	19
Importer	0.32	0.42	0.79	0.70	74

Sources: IEA; GTZ; country authorities; Thompson Reuters; and IMF staff estimates.

Note: Net tax measures the gap between domestic retail prices and international spot prices, adjusted for transportation and distribution margins. A pass-through of 1 would imply that the unit fuel tax level remains constant.

Medium-Term Outlook

Following a substantial tightening in advanced economies in 2012, consolidation efforts on current policies will wind down over the medium term, leaving headline and cyclically adjusted deficits in excess of precrisis levels. Countries delaying adjustment in 2011 will face more significant challenges to meet their medium-term objectives.

In the *advanced economies*, extraordinary adjustment efforts are on tap for 2012. Deficits are projected to fall by about 2 percent of GDP in the advanced economies, the largest aggregate decline in at least 40 years (Figure 1.10). In the United States, the FY2012 budget announced in mid-February maintains the president's commitment to halve the federal deficit by the end of his first term and the authorities' Toronto Group of Twenty (G-20) commitment to halve the 2010 deficit by 2013. The president's draft budget implies a major cyclically adjusted withdrawal of about 4 percentage points of GDP in FY2012. While in the United Kingdom the deficit reduction will be in line with that of 2011, in the euro area the pace of deficit reduction is projected to slow, after implementation of heavily front-loaded plans in many countries in 2009–11. However, the recent agreement in the EU to set a numerical benchmark for debt reduction for countries whose debt ratios exceed 60 percent—a reduction by one-twentieth in the gap between their level of debt and the threshold—could imply a somewhat faster pace of consolidation in several countries.

On current plans, deficit reduction in advanced economies will slow in 2013 and largely cease in 2014, leaving deficits above precrisis levels in several of them (Table 1.4; Statistical Table 1). Japan and the United States, in particular, are projected to record 2016 deficits that exceed their 2007 levels by at least 3 percent of GDP. The 2016 deficit is also projected above its precrisis level in Italy, by a smaller amount. Deficits in 2016 are expected to be close to precrisis levels in Germany and substantially below precrisis levels in France and the United Kingdom. The gross general government debt ratio is projected to peak at 107 percent of GDP in 2016, some 34 percentage points above its precrisis level (Figure 1.11; Statistical Table 7). The modest downward revision in the medium-term debt ratio compared with the

Figure 1.10. Advanced Economies: General Government Primary Balance
(Percent of GDP)

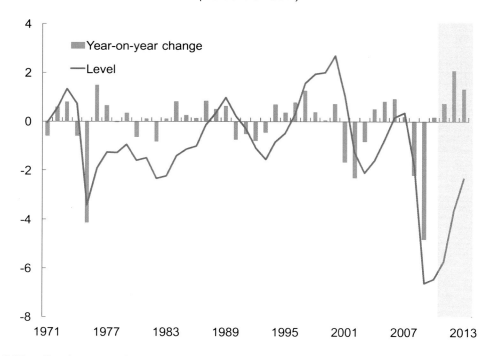

Source: IMF staff estimates and projections.

Note: Weighted average (GDP at PPP) for the advanced economies, with moving weights. Excludes financial sector support in the United States. Shaded areas denote projections.

Table 1.4. Medium-Term Projections
(Percent of GDP)

	2000–07	2007	2016
Overall Balance			
Advanced Economies	-2.0	-1.1	-3.5
Emerging Economies	-2.1	-0.1	-1.2
Cyclically Adjusted Balance			
Advanced Economies	-2.1	-1.6	-3.3
Emerging Economies	-2.2	-1.1	-1.6
Cyclically Adjusted Primary Balance			
Advanced Economies	-0.2	0.2	-0.4
Emerging Economies	0.4	1.2	-0.0
Gross General Government Debt			
Advanced Economies	71.0	73.1	107.3
Emerging Economies	43.1	36.0	30.1

Sources: IMF staff estimates and projections.

Figure 1.11. General Government Gross Debt Ratios

(Percent of GDP; 2009 PPP-GDP weighted averages)

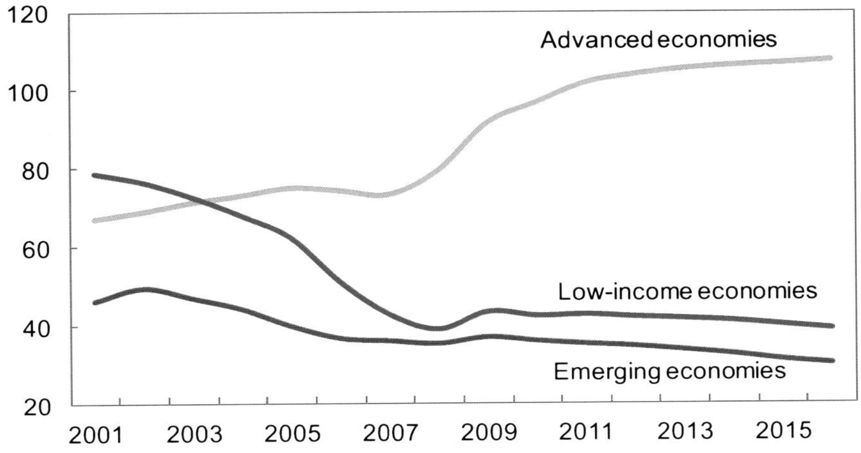

Sources: IMF staff estimates and projections.

November 2010 *Fiscal Monitor* reflects a slightly better than projected outturn in 2010 as well as somewhat more optimistic projections for the interest rate–growth differential in the years ahead. Although most fiscal adjustment is planned to come from the spending side (November 2010 *Fiscal Monitor*), public spending as a share of GDP is projected to remain close to 3 percent of GDP over its precrisis level in the medium term in advanced economies (Statistical Table 5).

For *emerging economies*, the baseline medium-term scenario remains benign. The average headline deficit for emerging economies is projected to fall by ½ percent of GDP in 2012, one-third the reduction in 2011. Under current projections, the average deficit for emerging economies is expected to converge to 1¼ percent of GDP by 2016, compared to rough balance prior to the crisis. The average debt-to-GDP ratio is expected to ease to 30 percent of GDP in 2016, below both historical averages and precrisis levels. However, this decline stems primarily from prospects of favorable growth and relatively low interest rates, as primary balances are expected to remain weak (see Chapter 3 for a discussion of the related fiscal risks).

In *low-income economies*, fiscal balances are expected to return to precrisis levels over the medium term, rebuilding the buffers that mitigated the impact of the crisis. Fiscal adjustment in the medium term will gradually reverse the countercyclical policies implemented during the crisis. Among noncommodity and commodity exporters, deficit reductions are expected to be achieved through continued revenue growth. Among fuel exporters, spending moderation will also be required as the short-term boost in oil revenues dissipates. General government gross debt is expected to stabilize at close to 40 percent of GDP, below precrisis levels.

Longer-Term Adjustment Needs

Especially in advanced economies, substantial further adjustment will be required over the remainder of the decade to eventually restore debt ratios to prudent levels. The challenge is even greater when the impact of trends affecting entitlement spending is taken into account. Indeed, rising spending on health care is the main risk to fiscal sustainability, with an impact on long-run debt ratios that, absent reforms, will dwarf that of the financial crisis. Even with reforms, entitlement spending pressures in some countries are likely too large to be fully contained, and offsetting measures will be needed elsewhere. In many emerging and low-income economies the challenge will be to improve coverage of health and pension systems in a fiscally sound manner.

In *advanced economies*, longer-term adjustment needs remain large. The customary illustrative exercise conducted in the *Fiscal Monitor* reports the level to which the cyclically adjusted primary balance must improve by 2020, and subsequently be maintained until 2030, for advanced economies to gradually reduce their debt to 60 percent of GDP (approximately the median precrisis level) by 2030 (Table 1.5a) (40 percent for emerging economies, also the median precrisis level) (Table 1.5b). On average, the required improvement in the cyclically adjusted primary balance between 2010 and 2020 amounts to about 8 percent of GDP. The necessary measures rise to about 12 percent of GDP when one takes into account the projected increase in age-related spending between 2010 and 2030 (Statistical Table 9).

Required adjustment exceeds 5 percent of GDP in one-third of the advanced economies. Japan, Ireland, the United States, and Greece all confront adjustment needs of 10 percent of GDP or more. For Japan and Ireland, the challenge stems from large current deficits combined with the need to run large future surpluses to service a sizable debt. For the United States, the pressure comes from the large deficit. For Greece, considerable progress has already been made in reducing the primary deficit, but significant further adjustment is needed to stabilize and then reduce the debt ratio. Compared with the November 2010 *Fiscal Monitor*, adjustment needs have been revised notably upward for Greece, New Zealand, and Portugal and downward for Austria, Belgium, Canada, Finland, and the Netherlands.

These adjustment needs are sensitive to assumptions about interest rate–growth differentials and about the extent to which past stimulus will be automatically reversed. The assumption of a uniform long-term interest rate–growth differential r–g in the baseline exercise (Table 1.5a; Figure 1.12, panel a) may be unduly favorable to highly indebted countries because it ignores the impact of high debt on growth and interest rates (see also Chapter 3). Using country-specific differentials that are assumed to be positively linked to countries' debt ratios, adjustment needs increase by 2 percent of GDP in Greece and Japan and by 1 percent in Italy. By contrast, in most advanced economies, the 2010 cyclically adjusted primary balance includes temporary discretionary stimulus measures. Assuming these measures are unwound upon expiration (Figure 1.12, panels c and d) reduces additional adjustment needs significantly in the United States, Japan, and Germany.

Although substantial fiscal consolidation remains in the pipeline, adjustment will need to be stepped up in most advanced economies, especially to offset the impact of age-related spending. The average projected adjustment of 3½ percent of GDP between 2010 and 2016 amounts to less than half that needed through 2020. Post-2016 gaps are larger than 3 percent of GDP for several advanced economies, including Belgium, Ireland, Japan, Spain, and the United States. Thanks to stronger planned adjustment, Germany is projected to implement the required adjustment by 2014 (Figure 1.13). Korea's cyclically adjusted primary balance already exceeds that needed to achieve its illustrative debt target, while in a few advanced economies

Table 1.5a. Advanced Economies:
Needed Fiscal Adjustment—An Illustrative Scenario

(Percent of GDP)

	Current WEO Projections, 2010			Illustrative Fiscal Adjustment Strategy to Achieve Debt Target in 2030		
	Gross Debt	Primary Balance	Cyclically Adjusted PB	Cyclically Adjusted PB in 2020–30	Required Adjustment between 2010 and 2020	Required Adjustment and Age–Related Spending, 2010–30
Australia	22.3	-4.3	-4.2	0.1	4.3	7.7
Austria	69.9	-1.9	-0.9	1.5	2.4	6.7
Belgium	97.1	-1.3	0.4	3.4	3.1	8.7
Canada	84.0	-4.9	-3.4	0.9	4.4	7.9
Czech Republic	39.6	-3.9	-2.9	0.9	3.8	4.4
Denmark	44.3	-4.6	-3.2	0.9	4.2	6.2
Estonia	6.6	-0.3	3.5	0.0	-3.5	-3.1
Finland	48.4	-3.2	-0.2	0.7	0.9	6.6
France	81.8	-4.8	-3.2	3.0	6.2	8.4
Germany	80.0	-1.1	-0.3	1.9	2.2	4.4
Greece	142.0	-3.2	-3.1	7.4	10.5	14.0
Hong Kong SAR	4.6	4.9	5.0	-1.6	-6.6	...
Iceland	96.6	-2.5	5.0	2.2	-2.8	2.4
Ireland	96.1	-29.7	-6.1	6.3	12.4	14.4
Israel	77.9	-0.8	-0.8	0.9	1.7	...
Italy	119.0	-0.3	1.4	4.6	3.2	4.6
Japan	220.3	-8.4	-6.7	6.6	13.3	14.0
Korea	30.9	3.6	3.7	-0.7	-4.4	0.5
Netherlands	63.7	-3.7	-2.7	1.4	4.2	9.5
New Zealand	31.6	-4.9	-3.9	0.5	4.4	9.4
Norway	54.3	8.4	8.9	10.0	1.1	5.9
Portugal	83.3	-4.6	-3.1	3.3	6.4	10.6
Slovak Republic	42.0	-7.0	-6.1	0.9	7.0	8.9
Slovenia	37.2	-4.0	-2.7	1.0	3.7	7.7
Spain	60.1	-7.8	-6.3	1.9	8.2	10.3
Sweden	39.6	-1.2	0.0	0.3	0.3	0.6
Switzerland	55.0	0.7	0.8	0.2	-0.6	...
United Kingdom	77.2	-7.8	-5.9	3.4	9.3	13.5
United States	91.6	-8.9	-6.2	5.1	11.3	17.5
Average (PPP-weighted)	96.6	-5.9	-4.0	3.8	7.8	11.8
G-20	102.9	-6.4	-4.5	4.1	8.6	12.8

Sources: IMF staff estimates and projections.

Note: The table reports gross debt; CAPBs are reported in percent of nominal GDP (in contrast to the conventional definition in percent of potential GDP). General government data are used where available. In the illustrative fiscal adjustment strategy, the CAPB is assumed to improve in line with *Fiscal Monitor* projections in 2011–12 and gradually from 2013 until 2020; thereafter, it is maintained constant until 2030. The fifth column shows the CAPB adjustment needed to stabilize debt at the end-2012 level by 2030 if the respective debt-to-GDP ratio is less than 60 percent (no shading, "lower debt"), or to bring the debt ratio to 60 percent in 2030 (shaded entries, "higher debt"). The analysis is illustrative and makes some simplifying assumptions: in particular, up to 2015, an interest rate–growth differential of 0 percentage points is assumed, broadly in line with WEO assumptions, and 1 percentage point afterward regardless of country-specific circumstances. The last column adds the projected increase in health care and pension spending between 2010 and 2030 (see Statistical Table 9 and Appendix 1), which will require offsetting measures. Illustrative scenarios for Australia, Canada, Japan, and New Zealand are based on their net debt ratios (see Statistical Table 8 for net debt data); for Japan, a net debt target of 80 percent of GDP is assumed, which corresponds to a target of 200 percent of GDP for gross debt. For Norway, maintenance of primary surpluses at the projected 2012 level is assumed (primary balance includes oil revenue whereas elsewhere in this document the non-oil balance is shown). For the United States, the CAPB excludes financial sector support recorded above the line.

Table 1.5b. Emerging Economies:
Needed Fiscal Adjustment—An Illustrative Scenario

(Percent of GDP)

	Current WEO Projections, 2010			Illustrative Fiscal Adjustment Strategy to Achieve Debt Target in 2030		
	Gross Debt	Primary Balance	Cyclically Adjusted PB	Cyclically Adjusted PB in 2020–30	Required Adjustment between 2010 and 2020	Required Adjustment and Age-Related Spending, 2010–30
Argentina	47.8	1.5	0.9	0.5	-0.4	1.6
Brazil	66.1	2.4	2.4	1.5	-0.9	2.0
Bulgaria	18.0	-3.3	-0.6	0.1	0.7	1.6
Chile	8.8	-0.3	-1.9	0.3	2.2	...
China	17.7	-2.1	-2.4	0.3	2.7	3.7
Colombia	36.5	-1.0	-0.8	0.2	1.0	...
Hungary	80.4	-0.3	2.1	3.1	1.0	2.3
India	72.2	-4.7	-4.7	3.4	8.1	8.9
Indonesia	26.9	0.8	0.8	0.2	-0.6	0.2
Jordan	60.5	-3.0	-3.1	2.9	6.0	...
Kazakhstan	11.4	1.9	0.5	-0.4	-0.9	...
Kenya	50.5	-3.9	-3.1	1.6	4.7	...
Latvia	39.9	-6.5	-2.6	-0.1	2.5	4.4
Lithuania	38.7	-6.1	-4.4	1.6	6.0	9.2
Malaysia	54.2	-3.6	-3.9	2.5	6.4	8.8
Mexico	42.7	-1.8	-1.1	0.5	1.6	4.8
Morocco	49.9	0.5	0.6	1.9	1.3	...
Nigeria	16.4	-5.7	-5.6	-1.1	4.5	...
Pakistan	56.8	-1.6	-1.6	1.0	2.6	3.2
Peru	24.3	0.6	0.7	0.0	-0.7	...
Philippines	47.3	-0.1	0.0	0.5	0.5	1.5
Poland	55.7	-5.3	-5.1	2.1	7.2	7.6
Romania	35.2	-5.1	-4.0	0.4	4.4	7.6
Russia	9.9	-3.2	-1.5	0.2	1.8	7.5
South Africa	36.3	-3.1	-2.3	1.1	3.3	5.1
Thailand	43.3	-1.9	-1.6	0.8	2.3	...
Turkey	41.7	0.5	-0.6	0.0	0.6	5.1
Ukraine	40.5	-4.1	-1.7	0.7	2.3	9.5
Average (PPP-weighted)	36.5	-2.0	-1.9	1.0	2.9	4.5
G-20	35.2	-1.9	-1.8	1.0	2.8	4.8

Sources: IMF staff estimates and projections.

Note: In computing the primary balance, policy lending was excluded from primary expenditure. CAPBs are reported in percent of nominal GDP. In the illustrative fiscal adjustment strategy, the CAPB is assumed to improve in line with *Fiscal Monitor* projections in 2011–12 and gradually from 2013 until 2020; thereafter, the CAPB is maintained constant until 2030. The fifth column shows the CAPB adjustment needed to stabilize debt at the end-2012 level by 2030 if the respective debt-to-GDP ratio is less than 40 percent, or to bring the debt-to-GDP ratio to 40 percent in 2030. The analysis is illustrative and makes some simplifying assumptions: in particular, up to 2015, an interest rate–growth differential of 0 percentage points is assumed, broadly in line with WEO assumptions, and 1 percentage point afterward regardless of country-specific circumstances. For large commodity-producing countries, even larger fiscal balances might be called for in the medium term than shown in the illustrative scenario given the high volatility of revenues and the exhaustibility of natural resources. The last column adds the projected increase in health care and pension spending between 2010 and 2030 (Statistical Table 9), which will require offsetting measures. For Ukraine, the primary deficit excludes costs related to bank recapitalization and the gas utility.

Figure 1.12. Advanced Economies: Sensitivity Tests on Fiscal Adjustment Needs

(Percent of GDP)

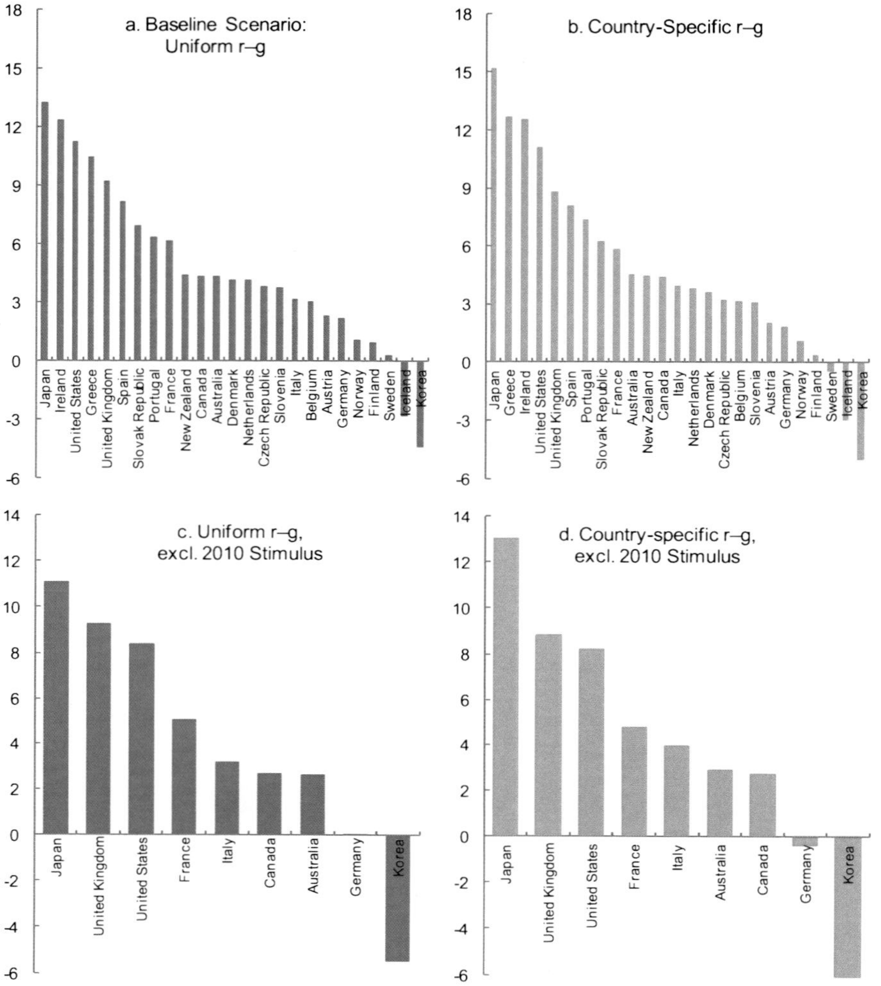

Sources: IMF staff estimates and projections.

Note: The baseline fiscal adjustment need for a uniform interest rate–growth differential across countries corresponds to the illustrative fiscal adjustment scenario depicted in Table 1.5a. The alternative scenario with country-specific interest rate–growth differentials uses country-specific projections for the interest rates (computed as the implied interest rate from fiscal interest expenditures) and GDP growth rates up to 2016. Afterward an interest rate–growth differential of 1 percent is assumed for the average of advanced economies, whereas country-specific differentials are determined as a function of their postcrisis (2016) indebtedness relative to the advanced economy average. Specifically, a country with a postcrisis debt ratio that is higher by 10 percentage points than the average is assumed to have a higher interest rate–growth differential by 0.25 percentage points, and correspondingly for countries with lower-than-average postcrisis indebtedness. The assumptions of a 1 percent average differential and a scaling factor of 0.25 are conservative compared to empirical estimates of the link between indebtedness and interest and growth rates outlined above. That is, this scenario illustrates possible developments under the premise of credible fiscal adjustment policies; with lower credibility (that is nonuniform across countries), interest rate–growth differentials would likely be higher (and more differentiated). Panels c and d show the adjustment needs excluding the impact of discretionary stimulus measures implemented during 2010; data on discretionary stimulus measures are from Box 1.1 of the November 2010 *Fiscal Monitor* and are available only for G-20 countries.

Figure 1.13. Selected Advanced Economies: Illustrative Adjustment Needs and Projected Fiscal Adjustment

(Percent of GDP)

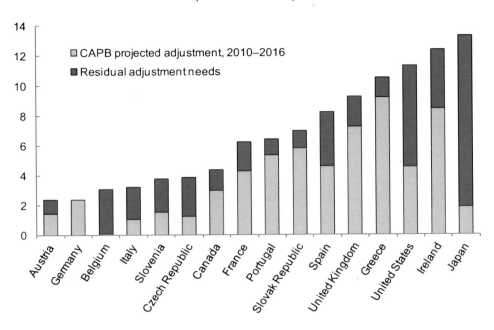

Source: IMF staff estimates and projections.

Note: The figure compares the estimated adjustment needs between 2010 and 2020 to achieve debt targets in 2030 (see note in Table 1.5a) and the projected change in the cyclically adjusted primary balance between 2010 and 2016 for the countries with positive residual adjustment needs beyond 2010. The 2010–16 projected adjustment exceeds illustrative needs in Australia, Denmark, Hong Kong SAR, Iceland, Israel, Korea, the Netherlands, New Zealand, Sweden, and Switzerland.

(including Australia, the Netherlands, New Zealand, and Sweden), planned adjustment exceeds calculated needs in this illustrative scenario.

In *emerging economies*, adjustment needs are generally smaller than in advanced economies, but with some important exceptions. Adjustment needs in emerging economies average about 3 percent of GDP. However, illustrative adjustment needs exceed 6 percent of GDP in India, Malaysia, and Poland. In Latvia and South Africa, the illustrative required adjustment is projected to be implemented and exceeded by 2016.

Figure 1.14. Public Health Spending in Advanced and Emerging Economies

(Percent of GDP)

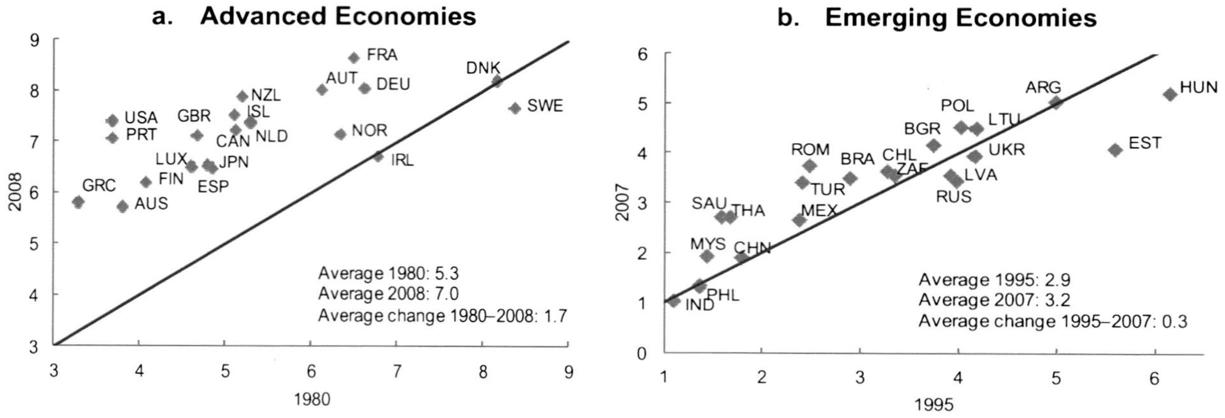

Sources: OECD Health Database; WHO; and IMF staff estimates.

Note: Sample periods for the advanced and emerging economies are chosen based on data availability. Data for 2008 refer to 2008 or latest year available. Averages are unweighted.

From an even longer-term perspective, spending on pensions—and especially, health care—constitutes a key challenge to fiscal sustainability. Over the past three decades, public spending on health care has risen rapidly in most advanced and emerging economies (Figure 1.14). Among advanced economies, health care spending growth has been more rapid in countries that started out with lower spending levels, as the result of "imitation" effects and technological diffusion of new health procedures (IMF, 2010a). Indeed, nondemographic factors such as rising income, technological advances, and health policies and institutions are the main reasons behind rising public spending-to-GDP ratios. New IMF staff projections suggest annual spending on public health will rise by an average of 3 percentage points of GDP in the advanced economies over the next 20 years, with an increase of 5 percent of GDP in the United States and 2 percent on average in Europe (Figure 1.15).[5]

---

[5] The projection for the United States is broadly consistent with U.S. Congressional Budget Office (CBO) projections incorporating the effects of the recent health care reform. The CBO projects increases in federally mandated spending (primarily Medicare and Medicaid) of 3½ percentage points of GDP in 2011–30. If other spending remains constant as a share of total public health spending, this implies increased spending of 5¼ percentage points of GDP. The projection for Europe exceeds the baseline projection of a ¾ percentage point of GDP increase over the next 20 years in the European Commission's (EC) Aging Report (European Commission, 2009). The EC projection assumes that technology will not increase costs, leading to excess cost

(continued)

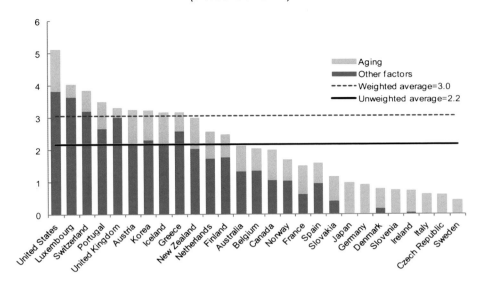

Figure 1.15. Advanced Economies: Projected Increases in Public Health Care Spending, 2011–30

(Percent of GDP)

Sources: OECD Health Database; and IMF staff estimates and projections.

The net present value of the flow of spending increases over the next 40 years is close to 100 percent of today's GDP, three times the estimated impact of the financial crisis on advanced economy public debt.

In view of these large projected increases in public health care spending, Appendix 1 analyzes experience with reform efforts and their potential impact. Unfortunately, recent reforms in advanced economies are unlikely to make a major dent in long-term trends.[6] International experience suggests

growth (ECG) of just 0.2 percent. This would represent a sharp break from past trends. For a fuller discussion of ECG and health care costs, see Appendix 1.

[6] In the United States, a sweeping reform expanding coverage is expected to reduce the budget deficit primarily because of higher payroll and excise taxes on health. The expected expenditure savings, however, are small and highly uncertain. In Europe, fiscal adjustment plans affecting general government employment and compensation could have an effect on health spending in the near term, but their long-term impact is uncertain. Reforms have also addressed spending on pharmaceuticals, which constitutes about 15 percent of public health spending. Recent reforms in advanced European economies (Germany, the United Kingdom), including those being undertaken in Greece as part of its fiscal adjustment program, have not been incorporated into the projections.

that there is scope to contain expenditure through greater use of market mechanisms, spending caps, supply constraints, price controls, and other reforms to slow the growth of spending. However, the impact of these reforms may still fall short of what is needed in some advanced economies to stabilize public health spending as a share of GDP. This means that further adjustment measures elsewhere in the budget will be required to control the growth of public spending. Compared to health care, medium-term pressures from pension spending appear more manageable, reflecting in part the impact of reforms that have already been implemented (IMF, 2010b).

2 Sovereign Financing and Government Debt Markets

At a Glance

Advanced economy financing needs will remain high, as increased rollover requirements offset lower deficits. By contrast, financing needs in emerging economies have fallen. With generally improved market confidence, the shortening of maturities witnessed at the outset of the financial crisis has been reversed. Interest rates have been rising in advanced economies, but the underlying causes—the economic recovery, inflation pressures, concerns about the cost of financial sector support—differ across countries. Markets are relatively sanguine about prospects for emerging market sovereigns.

Gross Financing Needs

After surging in 2010, gross financing needs in *advanced economies* are projected to rise somewhat further in 2011 and will remain high in 2012 (Table 2.1; Figure 2.1). Gradually declining deficits will be offset by rising debt rollovers from higher debt stocks and some maturity shortening early in the crisis. Japan has the highest requirement for 2011, at 56 percent of GDP, followed by the United States, Greece, Italy, Belgium, and Portugal at about half that level.

Table 2.1. Selected Advanced Economies' Gross Financing Needs, 2010–12

(Percent of GDP)

	2010			2011			2012		
	Maturing Debt	Budget Deficit	Total Financing Need	Maturing Debt	Budget Deficit	Total Financing Need	Maturing Debt[1]	Budget Deficit	Total Financing Need
Japan	43.4	9.5	52.9	45.8	10.0	55.8	44.4	8.4	52.5
United States	15.4	10.6	26.0	18.0	10.8	28.8	18.0	7.5	25.6
Greece	13.6	9.6	23.2	16.6	7.4	24.0	19.8	6.2	26.0
Italy	20.3	4.5	24.8	18.5	4.3	22.8	19.6	3.5	23.1
Belgium	17.8	4.6	22.4	18.5	3.9	22.4	18.6	4.0	22.6
Portugal	11.6	7.3	18.9	16.0	5.6	21.6	15.5	5.5	21.0
France	14.3	7.0	21.3	14.6	5.8	20.4	14.6	4.9	19.5
Spain	14.8	9.2	24.0	13.1	6.2	19.3	13.1	5.6	18.7
Ireland[2]	6.5	32.2	19.0	8.7	10.8	19.5	9.2	8.9	18.0
Canada	13.1	5.5	18.6	13.9	4.6	18.5	13.6	2.8	16.4
United Kingdom	5.3	10.4	15.7	7.1	8.6	15.7	6.7	6.9	13.6
Finland	9.1	2.8	11.9	10.0	1.2	11.2	8.6	1.1	9.7
Germany	8.5	3.3	11.8	9.1	2.3	11.4	9.0	1.5	10.5
Sweden	4.1	0.2	4.4	5.5	-0.1	5.4	5.0	-0.4	4.6
Australia	1.5	4.6	6.1	2.0	2.5	4.5	2.7	0.6	3.3
Weighted Average	17.2	8.7	25.8	18.9	8.1	27.0	18.7	6.1	24.8

Sources: Bloomberg; and IMF staff projections.

[1] Assumes that short-term debt maturing in 2011 will be refinanced with new short-term debt that will mature in 2012.

[2] Ireland's deficit in 2010 reflects the outlays on bank recapitalization, classified by the Irish authorities as expenditure, amounting to about €31 billion (20 percent of GDP). However, these outlays are in the form of promissory notes, do not require any upfront market financing, and therefore are not included in gross financing needs in 2010.

Figure 2.1. Advanced and Emerging Economies' Financing Needs, 2000–12

(Percent of GDP)

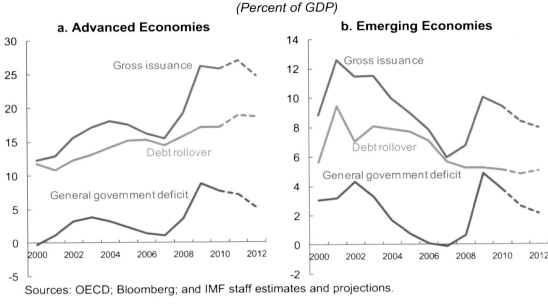

Sources: OECD; Bloomberg; and IMF staff estimates and projections.

Note: - - - denotes projections.

In contrast, financing needs in *emerging* and *low-income economies* are projected to decline in 2011–12, due to lower deficits and a lengthening of maturities. While there are pronounced cross-country differences, the average financing requirement in emerging economies is less than one-third that in the advanced economies (Figures 2.1 and 2.2), reflecting lower precrisis debt levels and smaller debt increases since 2007, as well as lower deficits.

A lengthening of debt maturities, after the decline early in the crisis, suggests some improvement in market confidence (Figure 2.3). The average maturity of government debt in advanced economies increased from 5½ years in April 2009 to 6½ years in December 2010. In the United States, the average maturity has also increased by about one year, more than reversing the drop at the onset of the crisis. With a few exceptions, countries with shorter maturities in 2009 succeeded in extending them, thus "locking in" historically low interest rates (Figure 2.4).[7] Although systematic data for domestic debt

---

[7] This trend may continue: the latest presentation of the Treasury Borrowing Advisory Committee suggests issuing bonds with maturities of up to 40–50 years which would be of interest to asset managers such as pension funds concerned with matching assets and liabilities. See United States, Department of Treasury (2011).

Figure 2.2. Emerging Economies: Gross Financing Needs, 2007 and 2011

(Percent of GDP)

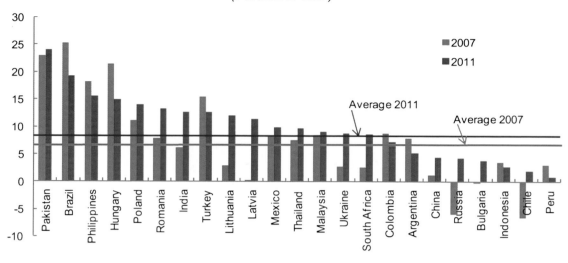

Source: IMF.

Figure 2.3. Advanced Economies: Average Maturity of Government Debt

(Years)

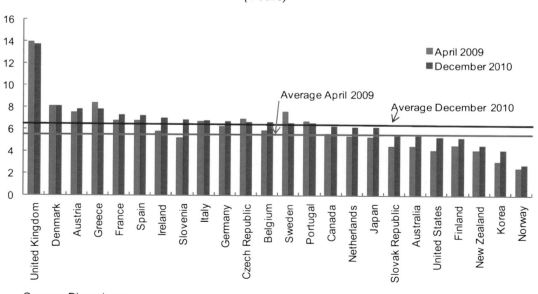

Source: Bloomberg.

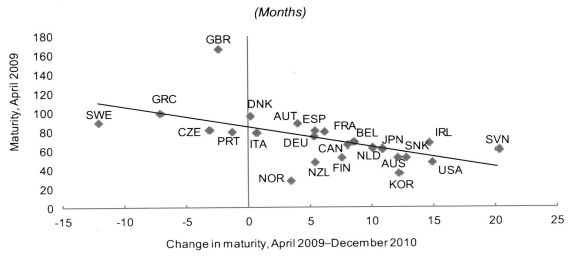

Figure 2.4. Advanced Economies: Change in Average Maturity

(Months)

Source: Bloomberg.

maturities are not available for emerging economies, international bond issuance suggests that average maturity began to increase in 2010, following a decline in 2008–09 that reflected a rise in risk aversion (Figure 2.5).

The share of nonresident holdings of government debt remained broadly stable in 2010, with a few exceptions. In Greece, nonresidents were net sellers of government debt, in spite of purchases by the European Central Bank (ECB), while domestic nonbank institutions increased their holdings. In Ireland, the earlier downward trend in the share of nonresident holdings—owing in part to a sharp increase in purchases of government debt by domestic nonbank financial institutions—reversed somewhat in 2010, although foreign demand continues to be subdued. The share of nonresident holdings in the United Kingdom has been rising since the Bank of England's withdrawal from the gilt market and the announcement of fiscal consolidation measures (Figure 2.6).

Figure 2.5. International Bond Issuance in Emerging Economies: Average Maturity

(Years)

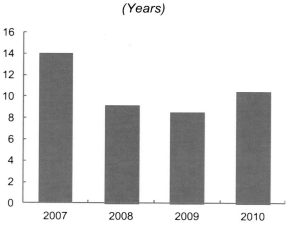

Source: Dealogic.

Figure 2.6. Advanced Economies: Marketable Central Government Debt Held by Nonresidents

(Percent of total outstanding marketable debt)

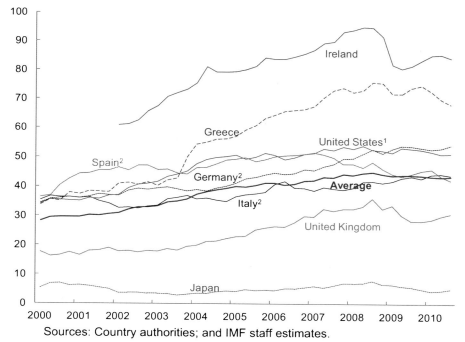

Sources: Country authorities; and IMF staff estimates.
Note: Data through 2010:Q3.
[1] Excluding Treasury bonds held by the Social Security Trust Fund.
[2] General government debt.

Sovereign Yields and Spreads

Better growth prospects are buoying advanced economy yields, but not all the news is good

Bond yields in *all major economies* have risen from low levels since late August (Figure 2.7, panel a). The synchronized upturn in yields coincided with a change in expectations regarding the global economic outlook following a strong signal of further quantitative easing (QE2) in the United States. The relative importance of different factors affecting interest rates varies across countries, however.

- In the *United States*, two opposing forces have been at play. First, improved growth prospects (April 2011 WEO) have been reflected in higher real yields (Figure 2.7, panel b), leading towards more normal interest rate levels. Inflationary expectations are also picking up, although they remain anchored (Figure 2.7, panel c).[8] Second, the additional easing from QE2 up to end-December, amounting to almost 56 percent of new net issuance in 2010:Q4 (Table 2.2), is likely to have lowered bond yields, other conditions being the same.[9] Credit default swap (CDS) spreads have been broadly flat, suggesting that solvency concerns have not played a role in the increase in bond yields.

- Improved growth prospects and rising inflationary expectations are also pushing up yields in *Germany* and *France* (Figure 2.8). With inflation above the ECB target, expectations of rate hikes are likely to have contributed to higher yields. A more positive economic sentiment also caused German real interest rates to rise in the past quarter, although 5-year real yields remain negative and 10-year real yields are still well below their

---

[8] Breakeven inflation rates over the 10-year horizon are around 2½ percent. Also, the U.S. Treasury yield curve has steepened since end-October 2010, which signals not only economic expansion, but also the possibility of inflation down the road—both pointing to rises in policy rates.

[9] It is difficult to make a precise quantification of the effect of QE2 but it is likely to be small and may primarily have occurred at the time of announcement (April 2011 GFSR).

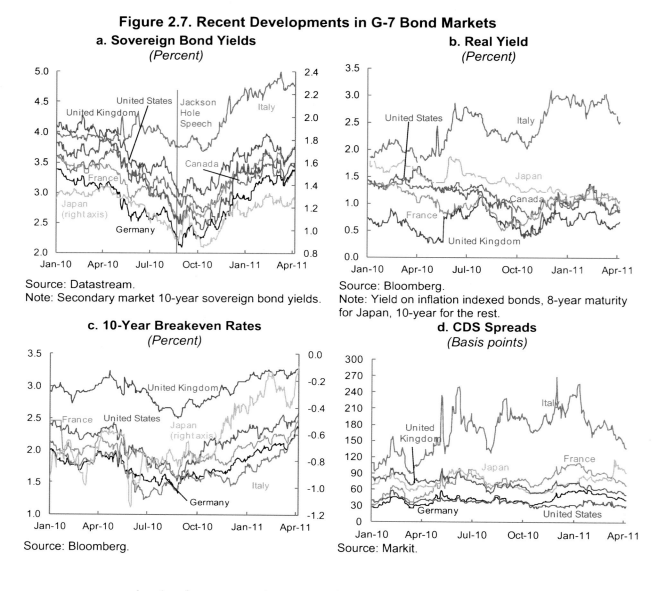

Figure 2.7. Recent Developments in G-7 Bond Markets

a. Sovereign Bond Yields
(Percent)

Source: Datastream.
Note: Secondary market 10-year sovereign bond yields.

b. Real Yield
(Percent)

Source: Bloomberg.
Note: Yield on inflation indexed bonds, 8-year maturity for Japan, 10-year for the rest.

c. 10-Year Breakeven Rates
(Percent)

Source: Bloomberg.

d. CDS Spreads
(Basis points)

Source: Markit.

levels of a year ago. A recent easing in CDS spreads in these two countries appears to reflect more favorable growth and fiscal developments (Figure 2.7, panel d). In *Italy*, CDS spreads have also come down, but remain elevated—indeed, twice as large as in other Group of Seven (G-7) countries.

Figure 2.8. Selected Advanced Economies: Change in Yields and Consensus Forecast

(Percentage points)

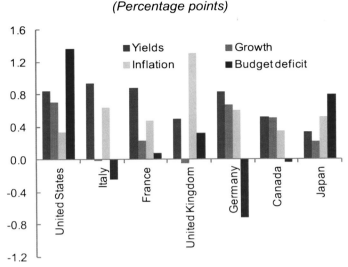

Sources: Bloomberg; and Consensus Forecast, Inc.

Note: Changes between October 2010 and March 2011. Consensus forecast for inflation, growth and the budget deficit refer to expectations for 2011. Change in inflation expectations is based on breakeven rates for France, Germany, Italy, and the United States; yields for 10-year benchmark bonds.

- In the *United Kingdom*, inflationary expectations appear to be a factor behind increases in nominal yields since the last quarter of 2010, as suggested by survey-based indicators (Figure 2.8). In contrast to the United States, quantitative easing did not play a role, as the Bank of England stopped its asset purchases in February 2010 (Table 2.2).

- In *Japan*, unlike other G-7 economies, increases in yields have been modest despite Standard and Poor's downgrading of the sovereign to AA–, and notwithstanding the catastrophic events following on from the earthquake in early March. This muted reaction is likely related to the stable domestic investor base (about 95 percent of Japanese bonds are owned domestically). Also, continued sluggish growth and deflation have

Table 2.2. Selected Advanced Economies: Central Bank Securities Holdings and Net Purchases, 2010

	Central Bank Holdings	Central Bank Purchases 2010			
		Q1	Q2	Q3	Q4
	(Percent of GDP)	(Percent of new net issuance)			
U.S. Federal Reserve					
Treasury Securities	6.9	0.0	0.1	8.9	55.6
Agency Debt and MBS[1]	7.8	...	...	...	...
European Central Bank					
Securities Market Program[2,3]	0.8	...	28.9	9.1	5.4
Bank of England					
Gilt Purchase under Asset Purchase Facility[3]	13.6	19.9	-0.3	-0.1	-0.3
Bank of Japan					
Japanese Government Securities[3]	16.0	20.0	5.3	24.3	0.2

Sources: Monetary authorities; IMF; and Haver.

[1] MBS=mortgage-backed securities.

[2] The ECB, statutorily, may purchase securities under this program only in the secondary market. In addition, the ECB purchased private-sector covered bonds totaling €60 billion under the Covered Bond Purchase Program from June 2009 to June 2010, mostly in the secondary market.

[3] Data on net issuance for 2010:Q4 are estimated.

played a role. The impact of securities purchases by the Bank of Japan in 2010:Q4 (Table 2.2) was negligible.[10] Nonetheless, CDS rates have started to edge up, somewhat more so in the aftermath of the earthquake, suggesting increased concern about the fiscal challenges facing the country.

Sovereign yields remain high in some euro area countries. Market reaction to the successful first bond placement of the European Financial Stability Facility (EFSF)—€5 billion in late January 2011—and the announcement of steps to strengthen the crisis management tools (including by raising the

---

[10] It is too early to assess the market impact of the Bank of Japan's decision to double the size of its Asset Purchase Program to ¥10 trillion following the March earthquake and ensuing events.

Figure 2.9. Recent Developments in Selected European Bond Markets

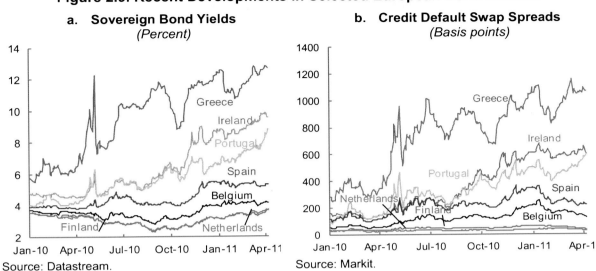

a. Sovereign Bond Yields
(Percent)

b. Credit Default Swap Spreads
(Basis points)

Source: Datastream.

Note: 10-year sovereign bond yields.

Source: Markit.

effective capacity of the EFSF to €440 billion and agreeing on the key parameters of the European Stabilization Mechanism [ESM] at the EU Summit in early March) has been moderately positive. However, market conditions remain tense in several smaller countries, in part due to ongoing concerns about possible feedback between the financial sector and the sovereign (April 2011 GFSR). Thus, following a short respite, yields have increased since end-January 2011 (Figure 2.9, panel a), with an uptick in the spreads over the German Bund of more than 50 basis points. At the same time, CDS spreads remain close to historical peaks (Figure 2.9, panel b). The ECB has continued its bond purchases under the Securities Market Program to stabilize markets, with outstanding holdings of bonds reaching €77 billion (Table 2.2). Although information on the country composition of ECB purchases is not publicly available, market observers believe that the ECB has preponderantly bought bonds from Greece, Ireland, and Portugal. If bonds from only these countries were bought, total ECB purchases during 2010 would have represented around 87 percent of the fiscal deficit in these countries.

Within Europe, investors are increasingly discriminating in favor of countries with credible policy frameworks. The dispersion in yields has exceeded the pre–European Monetary Union level, including during the European

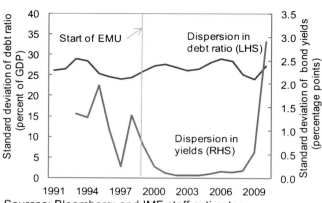

Figure 2.10. Euro Area: Variation in Yields and Debt Levels

Sources: Bloomberg; and IMF staff estimates.

Note: Countries included are France, Germany, Greece, Ireland, Italy, Spain, and Portugal.

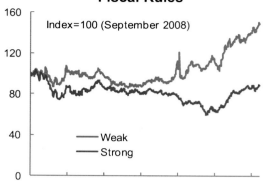

Figure 2.11. Euro Area: Average Yield and the Strength of Fiscal Rules

Sources: Bloomberg; and European Commission.

Note: Countries classified as strong are those where the fiscal rule strength index is above the median as of 2008. The sample includes all EU-15 countries except for Luxembourg.

Monetary System crisis of the early 1990s, even though cross-country variance in debt ratios has not increased much (Figure 2.10). The strength of fiscal institutions may play a role in these differences: euro area countries with stronger fiscal rules and medium-term budget frameworks had on average a 230-basis-point smaller increase in yields from the beginning of the crisis than did countries with weaker institutions (Figure 2.11).[11] Also, econometric analysis for a panel of 21 advanced economies shows that the effect of the fiscal position on financing costs is higher for countries rated below AAA (Jaramillo, 2011), suggesting that investors have less tolerance for slippages among countries lacking strong market credentials.[12]

Investor views of emerging markets are positive

Market perceptions of *emerging market* risk remain benign. With favorable market assessments of the growth outlook and fiscal conditions, EMBI and CDS spreads have remained broadly unchanged since October 2010

---

[11] Iara and Wolff (2010) suggest that yield spreads against Germany of countries with relatively weak fiscal rules could be up to 100 bps lower if they upgrade their numerical fiscal rules.

[12] For emerging markets, Jaramillo and Tejada (2011) find that reducing debt-to-GDP ratios lowers spreads significantly, especially for countries with lower sovereign credit ratings.

Figure 2.12. Emerging Markets: EMBI and Five-Year CDS Spreads
(Basis points)

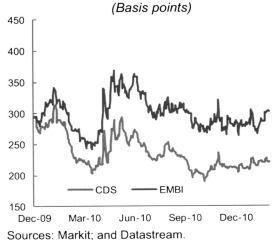

Sources: Markit; and Datastream.

Figure 2.13. Emerging Markets: EMBI Spreads by Region
(Basis points)

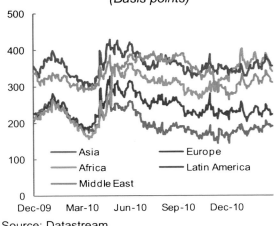

Source: Datastream.

Figure 2.14. Selected Emerging Markets: Change in Bond Yields and Inflation Expectations, October 2010–February 2011

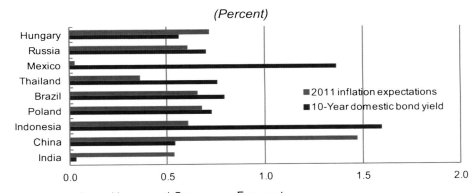

Sources: Bloomberg; Haver; and Consensus Forecast.

(Figure 2.12), with the exception of those for countries experiencing political turmoil, such as Côte d'Ivoire, Egypt, and Tunisia, or facing a markedly weaker fiscal outlook, such as Hungary (Figure 2.13). Spillovers to emerging economies from pressures in Ireland during November were limited and short-lived, even within Europe, in comparison to the market turbulence that followed the Greek crisis. The moderate increase in bond yields in domestic markets can be attributed to rising global interest rates, although in some cases higher inflation expectations—stemming from strong domestic demand and rising international commodity prices—have also been an important factor (Figure 2.14).

41

Shocks to the Baseline Fiscal Outlook

At a Glance

Deviations from the baseline fiscal outlook presented in Chapters 1 and 2 may occur as a result of macroeconomic, financial sector, and policy implementation shocks. In the period ahead, risks to fiscal developments arise particularly from two shocks. First, an increase in exceptionally low interest rates could complicate the budgetary outlook in both advanced and emerging economies. In some emerging markets, this risk is compounded by a possible reversal of the unusually supportive combination of high commodity prices and strong capital inflows. The second set of risks involves policy implementation shocks in some advanced economies.

Growth uncertainty is lower, but interest rate shocks remain a risk

The risks to the fiscal accounts arising from short-term output shocks have declined in both advanced and emerging economies.[13] As growth has picked up in many advanced economies, the risk of a "double-dip" recession appears to have declined, and the dispersion of analysts' real GDP forecasts has accordingly narrowed in recent months (Figure 3.1; April 2011 WEO). There are of course exceptions: with the ongoing political turmoil in the Middle East and North Africa, and the earthquake and ensuing events in

---

[13] Fiscal forecasts for both advanced and emerging economies are highly sensitive to growth assumptions. As a first approximation, each 1 percentage point increase in output growth would improve the annual fiscal balance by 0.4 percent of GDP in advanced economies and 0.3 percent of GDP in emerging economies.

Figure 3.1. Dispersion of One-Year-Ahead Real GDP Forecasts Across Analysts
(Percentile rankings)

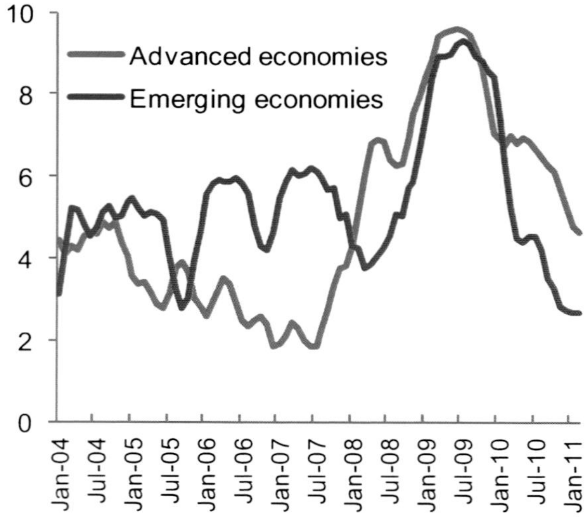

Sources: Consensus Forecast; and IMF staff calculations.
Note: Country groups are weighted to 2009 PPP-GDP weights.

Japan, new macroeconomic uncertainties have emerged for those areas. More generally, global downside risks stemming from higher oil prices have also increased and are not yet fully accounted for in most macroeconomic forecasts (April 2011 WEO).[14]

More sizable risks arise from interest rate shocks. Debt dynamics are critically affected by the interest rate–growth differential (IRGD). In the baseline projections discussed above, the IRGD is projected to remain low by historical standards over the medium term (Table 3.1). While still-weak economic activity makes this plausible, upside surprises cannot be ruled out.

---

[14] Leaving aside the uncertainty about short-term output growth, a significant source of uncertainty relates to whether potential output will recover its precrisis trend levels. For a discussion of the implications of this uncertainty for the fiscal accounts, see the May 2010 *Fiscal Monitor*, p. 20.

Table 3.1. Average Interest Rate–Growth Differential, 1990–2016

(Percentage points)

	1990–99	2000–10	2011–16
Advanced Economies	1.5	0.2	-0.4
G-7	3.2	1.6	-0.1
G-20 Advanced Economies	3.3	1.3	-0.3
Emerging Economies	-1.0	-3.3	-2.1
G-20 Emerging Economies	0.3	-3.0	-2.8
Low-Income Economies	-6.9	-7.3	-4.7

Source: IMF staff calculations.

Note: Adjusted for exchange rate effect. Data are not available for all countries for all years. Unweighted averages.

High debt ratios in many *advanced economies* leverage the impact of small interest rate shocks. Under a scenario in which interest rates on new debt issuances are 100 basis points higher than in the baseline, by 2016 the interest burden in advanced economies would increase by 1 percentage point of GDP on average (1¼ percentage points for the United States and 1½ percentage points for Japan; Figure 3.2).[15] If larger fiscal deficits resulting from this scenario were accompanied by a further increase in interest rates reflecting a risk premium, the effect on debt servicing costs could be even greater. For example, if rates were to rise an additional 20 basis points for each percentage point increase in a country's deficit-to-GDP ratio— consistent with the existing empirical evidence[16]—interest payments in 2016 would be 1½ percentage points of GDP higher than the original baseline on average (with increases of 1½ percentage points for the United States and 2 percentage points for Japan). (For some complementary interest rate sensitivity analyses, see the April 2011 GFSR.)

Lower debt ratios in *emerging markets* provide some protection from the impact of changes in the interest rate–growth differential, but the IRGD is

---

[15] For these calculations, gross financing needs are calculated assuming that the average maturity profile of each country remains the same as in 2010. The estimation also takes into account the impact on interest income.

[16] See, for instance, Baldacci and Kumar (2010).

Figure 3.2. Selected Advanced Economies: Budgetary Impact of Interest Rate Increases

(Percent of GDP)

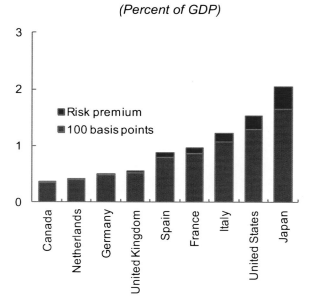

Source: IMF staff calculations.

nevertheless subject to strong medium-term uncertainty and to high short-term volatility in these countries. The baseline projections envisage a sharply negative IRGD in emerging economies, a critical factor explaining why debt dynamics in these economies remain favorable despite persistent negative primary balances over the medium term (Figure 3.3; Statistical Table 2). A negative IRGD is not unusual for emerging economies. Box 3.1 discusses some of the reasons why, noting the importance of financial underdevelopment and repression in driving down real interest rates (and hence the IRGD). These findings suggest that as financial systems in emerging markets develop and are liberalized, interest rates on public debt will likely increase, requiring in turn a strengthening of primary balances over time to keep debt ratios stable. The extent to which these developments will already be felt during the forecasting horizon is unclear, but higher pressure on interest rates is possible, especially as rates normalize in the advanced economies. The box also highlights the greater volatility of IRGD for

Figure 3.3. Emerging Markets: Budgetary Impact of Interest Rate Increases

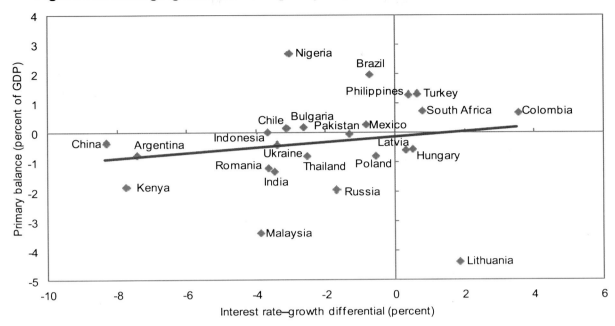

Source: IMF staff projections.

Note: Interest rate–growth differential is adjusted for exchange rate effect.

emerging than for advanced economies, another potential source of shocks to the baseline forecast.

In addition to low interest rates, the fiscal accounts of emerging economies are currently benefitting from additional tailwinds, although to different extents. As noted, the revenues of net exporters have been boosted by rising commodity prices. Asset price booms, spurred by capital inflows, are also raising revenues. Clearly, the more rapid the reversal of these favorable tailwinds, the more severe would be its impact on the fiscal accounts. In this respect, it is noteworthy that portfolio inflows—among the more volatile sources of foreign financing—represent a significant share of the recent increase in capital flows to emerging markets (April 2011 WEO).

The overall effects of a reversal of these favorable conditions on emerging economies could be sizable:

- Each 100-basis-point increase in interest rates on newly issued debt in emerging markets would raise annual interest payments by ½ percent of GDP on average by 2016.

- For a sample of nine emerging economies representing a cross-section of commodity exporters, a 10 percentage point across-the-board fall in commodity prices would lead to a decline of more than 1 percent of GDP in budget revenues annually.[17]

- A fall in equity prices that returns emerging economy indices to their precrisis levels (about 20 percent in real terms) would result, on average, in a decline of about ¼ percent of GDP in revenues.

The projected strengthening of overall balances in *low-income economies* is subject to several risks. These include uncertainty in grant disbursements given fiscal pressures in advanced economies; rising debt service costs; and pressure to increase spending on subsidies and public wages, especially for food and fuel importers. Commodity-exporting countries (for example, Angola, Bolivia, and Chad) also face the risk of an abrupt decline in commodity prices.

Advanced economy financial sectors have stabilized, but guarantees are still lurking

Financial sector risk has declined, but remains elevated in *advanced economies*.[18] Financial market performance has been favorable over the past six months, but balance sheet restructuring is still incomplete and is proceeding only slowly, with leverage remaining high (April 2011 GFSR). Although, as noted

---

[17] The countries included in the sample are Argentina, Chile, Colombia, Indonesia, Mexico, Nigeria, Peru, the Russian Federation, and Saudi Arabia. The calculation assumes no supply response to the change in global prices and is therefore intended only as a "ready reckoner" of the impact of a price fall.

[18] For a detailed discussion of remaining financial sector vulnerabilities, see the April 2011 GFSR.

in Chapter 1, the net direct cost of financial sector support has so far been lower than in past crises, risks remain high. Estimates of the net fiscal costs from past banking crises range widely, from close to zero in Sweden (where large gross costs were almost fully recovered, after several years) to more than 50 percent of GDP in the case of Indonesia. In the current crisis, the low direct cost thus far can be explained by the relatively limited use of public recapitalization schemes, partly reflecting the role played by the private sector in the restructuring of assets (Laeven and Valencia, 2010). As a counterpart, there has been wide use of guarantees, asset insurance, and liquidity support, which reduces the need for up-front fiscal outlays but increases risks going forward. One such item is especially large by historical standards: bonds issued by financial institutions with a government guarantee are estimated at over $1.25 trillion at end-2010 for a sample of advanced economies (Figure 3.4), equivalent to 6 percent of GDP for the countries in the sample. The magnitude of these potential further fiscal costs highlights the importance of a coherent strategy to restore banking sector viability, particularly in Europe.

For *emerging economies*, financial sector risk continues to be generally lower than for advanced economies but is broadly unchanged relative to six months ago. While financial market conditions have improved, large capital inflows and easy credit conditions pose risks to the financial system (through rapid credit growth and excessive risk taking) with possible implications for the budget.

Fiscal institutions are under stress in some countries, and political conditions do not favor bold policy action in others

Policy implementation shocks are hard to assess, but many advanced economies will face important challenges. A major adjustment would be

Figure 3.4. Selected Advanced Economies:
Volume of Outstanding Government-Guaranteed Bonds

($US billions)

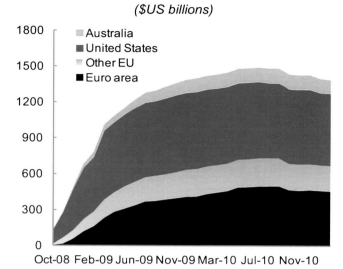

Sources: Dealogic; and IMF staff calculations.

Note: State guarantees on bonds issued by private and public banks and financial institutions. Short-term debt is not included.

needed in the United States in 2012 to put fiscal consolidation back on track (Chapter 1). Similar concerns apply to Japan, where increased spending due to the earthquake may lead to higher medium-term consolidation needs. Elsewhere, protracted delays in resolving uncertainties related to the European Financial Stability Facility and European Stabilization Mechanism put upward pressure on interest rates in some euro area economies. A failure to make adequate progress in resolving outstanding details (which is not in the baseline) risks triggering a sharp rebuke from bondholders. More broadly, there is a risk that the electoral calendar in the United States, France, and Japan, and possibly elsewhere, could complicate policy implementation. Experience with past consolidation episodes has shown that greater fractionalization in the legislature and perceptions of lower political stability are associated with weaker implementation of plans.

Strengthening fiscal institutions, including public financial management frameworks, fiscal rules, and fiscal councils, can reduce the risk of policy slippages. Regrettably, recent developments in this area are mixed:

- In Hungary, the nonpartisan independent fiscal agency was effectively closed. In contrast, however, a few advanced economies have strengthened their fiscal plans and institutions. For example, the United Kingdom approved legislation for the Office for Budget Responsibility and issued its Spending Review, which details medium-term spending. Greece adopted a new Fiscal Management Law, and Serbia adopted a Fiscal Responsibility Law. In France, plans for a fiscal rule have not yet been implemented.

- Fiscal transparency seems to be increasingly at risk in some countries. With fiscal results facing heightened scrutiny, there is a growing tendency for governments to enter into transactions that sacrifice fiscal transparency (and, in some cases, long-term fiscal health) to make short-run budget outturns appear more positive. Moves by Argentina and Hungary to renationalize previously privatized second-pillar pension schemes are one example of this phenomenon. Likewise, Ireland's bank crisis resolution entity has been designated as a private sector organization, even though nearly all of its expenses will be financed with government-guaranteed debt. Appendix 2 reviews other examples of accounting stratagems that make the fiscal accounts appear stronger than is actually the case. These include securitizations of future income streams (or accounts receivable) that make borrowing look like revenue, deferral of spending through public-private partnerships, and sales of financial assets that treat the current proceeds as revenue but take no account of the resulting loss of future dividends or interest payments. Fundamentally, a clear resolve on the part of national authorities to maintain transparent and accurate fiscal accounts is the only surefire way to prevent misleading accounting tricks: almost any rule or standard can be evaded if governments set out to do so. However, the temptation to participate in these types of transactions can be limited by ensuring that governments prepare their fiscal accounts according to broadly accepted principles and use as wide a definition of the public sector as feasible. More can be done to encourage compliance with standards, as well.

Box 3.1. Debt Dynamics and the Interest Rate–Growth Differential

For decades, a negative interest rate–growth differential has been a feature of most emerging and low-income economies (first figure). Statistical evidence indicates that the IRGD is strongly correlated with the level of economic development. It is positive (averaging about 1 percent) for G-20 advanced economies and negative for emerging economies (about –4 percent) and lower-income countries (about –8 percent).

Economic theory does not offer any obvious reason for this marked correlation, since both growth and interest rates should normally be higher in emerging and low-income economies than in advanced ones. In practice, however, real interest rates in these economies are generally *lower* than in advanced economies (and often are largely negative), and this is the main cause of negative IRGDs. In the case of developing economies, both econometric and qualitative evidence suggest that negative real rates on domestic debt are due to a lack of financial development and to financial repression and distortions, including captive domestic markets for government debt, directed lending, and government involvement in credit markets (second figure).

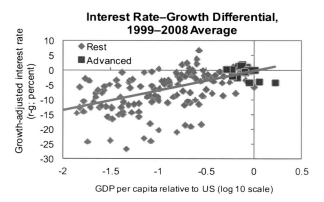

Interest Rate–Growth Differential, 1999–2008 Average

Sources: Country authorities; and IMF staff estimates and projections.
Note: Includes currency valuation effects.

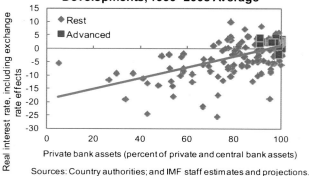

Real Interest Rates and Financial Developments, 1999–2008 Average

Sources: Country authorities; and IMF staff estimates and projections.

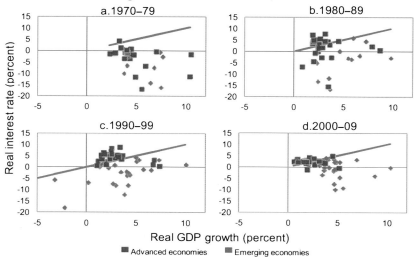

Rising Real Interest Rates in Recent Decades

a.1970–79

b.1980–89

c.1990–99

d.2000–09

Real interest rate (percent)

Real GDP growth (percent)

■ Advanced economies ■ Emerging economies

Sources: Country authorities; and IMF staff estimates and projections.
Note: Country sample is based on data availability. Advanced economies are defined as in the *Fiscal Monitor* with the exception of Slovenia and the Slovak Republic, which were not members of the Organization for Economic Cooperation and Development during most of the analyzed period.

Box 3.1 *(concluded)*

An array of financial development and capital account openness indicators are positively correlated with the IRGD, mainly through their impact on interest rates, while their relation with growth is weaker. In particular, high inflation and the apparent inability of investors to incorporate it into nominal interest rates (or shift investment to alternative assets with positive real returns) appear to have been instrumental in driving down real interest rates on government debt. High savings rates have also often contributed (Escolano, Shabunina, and Woo, 2011).

If so, it would be a mistake to assume that negative IRGD will persist over the long term, and indeed real interest rates have been rising in emerging markets since the 1990s in parallel with financial globalization and increasingly integrated international financial markets (third figure, on preceding page). This process also occurred in advanced economies during the financial liberalization and capital market deepening of the 1980s (fourth figure). Declines in saving rates or broader domestic investment opportunities would add to this process.

Real Interest Rates and Financial Reform Index

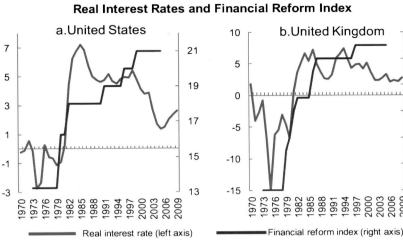

Sources: Country authorities; and IMF staff estimates and projections.

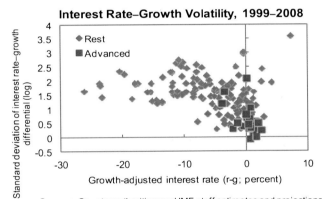

Sources: Country authorities; and IMF staff estimates and projections.
Note: Includes currency valuation effects.

Moreover, even in the short term, unsound underlying fiscal positions can result in pronounced abrupt changes in the IRGD of emerging and developing economies. Within-country IRGD volatility is substantially higher (and IRGD persistence lower) for economies with lower income and IRGDs—increasing debt dynamics uncertainty (fifth figure).

4 Assessing and Mitigating Fiscal Sustainability Risks

At a Glance

This section summarizes risks to fiscal sustainability and discusses policy options to address them. The analysis draws on earlier chapters, complemented by more formal analysis based on fiscal indicators (see also Appendix 3). It tries to determine how the risk of a fiscal crisis of regional or systemic relevance has changed with respect to the assessment provided in the November 2010 Fiscal Monitor.

How Have Fiscal Sustainability Risks Changed?

There has been limited progress in reducing fiscal sustainability risks. For advanced economies, risks remain high overall, and the divergence across countries has increased since the November 2010 Fiscal Monitor. *In many emerging economies, headline fiscal positions are improving, but the underlying fiscal stance is often loose, which could pose a risk in the presence of shocks.*

Baseline trends remain weak, especially in advanced countries.

- Short- and medium-term fiscal trends remain weak in advanced economies but have improved somewhat in emerging economies. The ongoing consolidation in the euro area and the United Kingdom has occurred at a time of a further weakening of the fiscal position in Japan and the United States. Given these diverging trends, the baseline outlook for advanced economies is on average broadly unchanged compared to six months ago, with risks remaining high (Table 4.1). This is borne out by an analysis of numerical indicators compiled for the Fiscal Sustainability Risk Map in Appendix 3.[19] For emerging economies, baseline projections have on average improved somewhat. The indicator analysis confirms that although the overall level of risk has eased, it remains high by historical standards, with cyclically adjusted primary deficits above precrisis levels.

- Long-term spending pressures, which are broadly unchanged, remain significant. The risk profile (Table 4.1) reflects limited entitlement reforms. Recent pension reforms in France and Spain contribute to ameliorating long-term spending trends in these economies, but the impact on risk indicators for the advanced economies as a whole is marginal. For emerging economies, the stable baseline of long-term fiscal challenges reflects no significant change in entitlement policies in recent months. Spending pressures are in general lower than for advanced economies, with a key challenge being to improve coverage without incurring unsustainable fiscal costs.

- Risks related to the structure of liabilities have on average remained stable in advanced economies but have declined in emerging economies. Financing needs have increased in some advanced economies, including in the United States, despite a general lengthening of debt maturities. This has been partially offset by lower financing needs in many euro area countries owing to lower deficits. Altogether, this risk dimension is little changed (Table 4.1), as confirmed by the statistical indicators in Appendix 3. For emerging economies, the somewhat lower risk profile reflects a reduction in gross financing needs and a decline in the ratio of short-term external debt to reserves, as many of these economies experienced a rapid recovery in exports and capital inflows.

---

[19] The results of the indicators analysis reflect a worsening in the debt indicator, a small improvement in the cyclically adjusted primary balance indicator, and some worsening in the interest rate–growth differential.

Table 4.1. Assessment of Fiscal Sustainability Risks

	Advanced Economies	Emerging Economies
Short- and Medium-Term Fiscal Indicators	⟷	↘
Long-Term Fiscal Challenges	⟷	⟷
Liability Structure	⟷	↘
Macroeconomic Uncertainty	↘	↗
Financial Sector Risks	↘	⟷
Policy Implementation Risk	↗	⟷

Source: IMF staff calculations.

Note: Directional arrows ↔, ↑, and ↓ indicate on average unchanged, higher, or lower risks, respectively; ↗ and ↘ indicate moderate increases or decreases, respectively, in levels of risk.

Risks of shocks to the baseline have moved in divergent directions, but generally remain elevated.

- Uncertainty over output growth has eased for advanced economies. For emerging economies, however, where tailwinds have supported positive developments, vulnerability to negative shocks is reflected in an uptick in uncertainty. Concerns about inflationary pressures, as well as the uncertainties associated with the political turmoil in some countries in the Middle East and North Africa, have increased this risk factor. A key source of risk for both groups of countries relates to short- and medium-term developments in regard to interest rates.

- Financial sector risk in advanced economies remains elevated but has receded somewhat in recent months. Financial market performance has been favorable thus far in 2011, but balance sheet restructuring is still incomplete, and financial sector leverage and private sector indebtedness are still at high levels (April 2011 GFSR). Financial risk indicators (including the GFSR's Global Financial Stability Map indicators;

Appendix 3) point to financial sector risks being high but gradually falling thanks to a more stable market environment. In emerging economies, the beneficial impact of buoyant domestic financial markets and spillovers from the improved environment for advanced economies is counterbalanced by uncertainties emanating from rapid credit growth in some countries, resulting in an overall unchanged assessment for this indicator.

- Policy implementation risk has increased somewhat in the last six months (Chapter 3). The numerical indicators point to a deterioration in this dimension in advanced economies, based on an assessment of the quality of countries' adjustment plans, the major adjustment efforts implied by the baseline in some large countries, and political developments impinging on policy implementation (including the electoral cycle).

Measures to Mitigate Fiscal Sustainability Risks

Key advanced economies need to accelerate the adoption of credible fiscal consolidation measures and finalize the details of the crisis resolution frameworks. For many emerging economies, rebuilding fiscal buffers to deal with a potential reversal of the current benign conditions is a priority. Many low-income economies need to continue improving their fiscal positions while financing growth-enhancing initiatives in a sustainable manner.

Among the *advanced economies*, the United States, in particular, needs to adopt measures that would allow it to meet its fiscal commitments. Market concerns about sustainability remain subdued in the United States, but a further delay of action could be fiscally costly, with deficit increases exacerbated by rising yields. Rollover problems for the largest advanced economies remain a tail risk, but one that would entail huge costs for them and the rest of the world. In the United States, the additional fiscal stimulus planned for 2011 means that meeting President Obama's commitment to halve the federal deficit by the end of his first term would require an adjustment of 5 percentage points of GDP over FY2012–13, the largest in at least half a century. Given cyclical conditions, a down payment in the form of a reduction of the deficit for FY2011 that made the FY2013 objective compatible with a less abrupt withdrawal of stimulus later would be preferable. A commitment to a medium-term debt target as an anchor for fiscal policy would also be welcome. In Japan, the Fiscal Management Strategy envisages maintaining stable reductions in the debt ratio from FY2021. Once the fiscal costs of recent developments are assessed, commitment to a fiscal policy leading to a more rapid adjustment, supported by fiscal measures more clearly identified than in the past, would be appropriate.

In the euro area, fiscal adjustment is proceeding at the right pace, but a paramount objective is to agree on all aspects of a comprehensive pan-European approach to crisis management. The EFSF and the ESM must have the ability to raise sufficient resources quickly at low costs and to deploy them flexibly (April 2011 WEO). Recent progress is welcome, but some details will need to be finalized (see Box 4.1 regarding the recent decisions on the EFSF and the ESM and for more details on the fiscal aspects of the EU governance reforms). To increase the credibility of fiscal consolidation, those countries that have come under renewed market pressure need to stand ready to adopt additional measures to avoid slippages. More generally, several EU countries still need to specify and adopt appropriate policy measures to achieve the commitments within their stability and convergence programs. Efforts should be underpinned by strong national fiscal frameworks with minimum standards to be outlined by the European Commission, as well as structural reforms to boost growth.[20]

In general, *advanced economies* should respond flexibly to macroeconomic conditions. In all advanced economies, should growth turn out to be faster than projected in the WEO baseline, additional revenues should be saved. Should growth prove slower than currently projected, those advanced economies with fiscal space should let the automatic stabilizers operate.

---

[20] See the May 2011 *Regional Economic Outlook: Europe* (IMF, 2011c) and Allard and Everaert (2010) for a review of structural reform needs in Europe.

Box 4.1. Fiscal Aspects of EU Economic Governance Reforms

On March 24–25, the European Council endorsed several reforms aimed at enhancing policy coordination in the European Union. A final package is expected to take effect by June 2011, after negotiations with the European Parliament. The reforms enhance both the prevention and management of sovereign debt crises through:

- Broader policy coordination based on a European semester—which establishes an ex ante peer review of member states' fiscal and structural reform plans prior to the finalization of national budgets—and the Euro Plus Pact, which formalizes an agreement among euro area members to make specific commitments to strengthen competitiveness and convergence.

- A revamped Stability and Growth Pact (SGP): this reform goes a long way in addressing loopholes in fiscal surveillance. First, the reform introduces new sanctions, including deposits amounting to 0.2 percent of GDP in the preventive arm of the pact and fines of the same amount in the corrective arm. Decisions about these new sanctions will be subject to a reverse-majority mechanism by which the Council can only overrule the Commission with a qualified majority. Second, fiscal surveillance would be strengthened through a cap on growth in public spending net of discretionary revenue measures to encourage saving revenue windfalls. Third, the debt criterion in the corrective arm would be operationalized through a minimum debt reduction threshold to be met in addition to the 3 percent deficit ceiling.

- A directive to make (or adopt) rules-based national fiscal frameworks compatible with the SGP. This is important to encourage member states to take greater ownership of the common rules and improve their implementation, including by mandating transparent accounting, prudent forecasting and medium-term planning. Since a directive can only provide general guidelines, the commitment included in the Euro Plus Pact to adopt binding national rules is welcome.

- A new excessive imbalances procedure (EIP) to deal with macroeconomic imbalances. The EIP—which incorporates a preventive and a corrective arm—recognizes that unsustainable public debts may be rooted in nonfiscal problems—private sector financial excesses, eventually compounded by the realization of implicit or contingent liabilities.

- A permanent crisis management procedure. Crisis management will fall under the responsibility of a new institution, the European Stability Mechanism. The ESM essentially makes permanent the existing, strictly conditional assistance scheme (European Financial Stabilization Facility) and expands its instruments (bond purchases in the primary market). It will be helpful in preventing liquidity problems from casting doubts on a member state's capacity to fulfill its obligations. The effective financing available to the EFSF is also to be increased.

These reforms are an important step forward to encourage fiscal responsibility and prevent the recurrence of sovereign stress. However, some areas of concern persist. First, implementing some of the new SGP rules may prove challenging, in particular, when accounting for cyclical factors in the operation of the debt rule. Second, elements of the reforms need to be clarified, especially those relating to the EIP. Third, some aspects of SGP governance have not been reformed. In particular, the standard decision-making process—whereby the Council's qualified majority is needed, with abstentions effectively amounting to a negative vote—still applies to the key surveillance decisions, including the initiation of the excessive deficit procedure and the imposition of sanctions already envisaged under the old SGP.

Even though headline balances in *emerging economies* continue to improve, several considerations suggest that many need to adopt a more cautious fiscal policy. First, favorable tailwinds boosting revenues and containing spending may be short-lived. This is borne out by the experience of many European economies in the run-up to the recent crisis. Second, fiscal buffers were eroded by the crisis and should be rebuilt to protect against sudden reversals in capital inflows. Third, overheating concerns are increasing. In some emerging economies, particularly in Europe, that still face relatively high debt levels and the risk of spillovers from market pressures elsewhere, the need to improve fiscal positions is particularly urgent. These considerations suggest that, at a minimum, spending pressures should be resisted and automatic stabilizers allowed to come into play, thus enabling revenue overperformance to be saved in full. In countries where higher commodity prices are raising outlays on food and energy subsidies, better-targeted measures to protect the poor are needed.

For *low-income economies*, a key policy priority is to finance growth-enhancing initiatives without jeopardizing fiscal sustainability. The improvement in overall balances in low-income economies is welcome and will help rebuild fiscal buffers. Moreover, given large infrastructure gaps as well as the need to achieve the Millennium Development Goals, increased spending will be needed in the years ahead on public investment, education, and well-targeted transfer programs. To ensure that higher spending is financed in a sustainable manner without crowding out private investment, greater revenue mobilization—beginning with improved tax administration and wider tax bases—will be essential. In addition, reforms to strengthen public financial management would improve the quality of expenditures, including for public infrastructure, and thus their impact on economic growth (IMF, 2010c).

An analysis of past episodes of attempted large fiscal adjustments provides guidance regarding pitfalls to avoid and keys to success in fiscal consolidation. Appendix 4 summarizes the results of a detailed narrative analysis of 21 attempted large fiscal adjustment episodes in the G-7 countries and a cross-country statistical analysis of 66 large fiscal adjustment plans in European Union members over the past few decades. The focus on planned—rather than just successful—adjustment efforts allows the analysis to identify not only what policies aided deficit reduction, but also what policies failed.

Among the episodes analyzed, powerful shocks, especially to economic growth, often resulted in sizable deviations of fiscal outcomes from plans, thus highlighting the importance of spelling out up front how policies will respond. Plans need to incorporate explicitly mechanisms to deal with unforeseen circumstances, permitting some flexibility while credibly preserving medium-term consolidation objectives. Examples of helpful mechanisms include multiyear spending limits or, where feasible, cyclically adjusted fiscal targets. Contingency reserves also helped ensure successful outcomes: the creation of such reserves—or of backup measures to be implemented in the event that shortfalls begin to emerge—would be especially critical in economies under close market scrutiny, which have limited margin for error.

Although most adjustment programs evaluated aimed primarily at expenditure reduction, the latter often did not materialize, and in several cases deficit objectives were salvaged by revenue overperformance.[21] This suggests that countries that are planning primarily expenditure-based adjustments need to ensure that expenditure ceilings are adhered to by devising institutional mechanisms and implementing supporting structural reforms—key factors for success of past fiscal consolidations. In addition, countries would do well to consider supplementary, high-quality options on the revenue side, to be deployed in the event of expenditure overruns (IMF, 2010b).

Ideally, revenue increases would be achieved by widening tax bases and removing distortions, rather than by raising tax rates. In many countries, the elimination of tax expenditures can contribute to this objective. As noted in Appendix 5, the use of tax expenditures has grown significantly in recent

---

[21] As noted in the November 2010 *Fiscal Monitor*, most countries that have announced medium-term deficit reduction plans in response to the most recent financial crisis are also relying on expenditure measures.

years, and foregone revenues associated with such expenditures are estimated at 5 percent of GDP or more in many countries. Although tax expenditures can serve worthwhile goals—such as encouraging investment in particular industries or activities like research, or stimulating individuals to consume merit goods (like education) or to make charitable donations—policy objectives would in many cases be better served by a more transparent allocation of government resources (for example, via a direct subsidy from the budget rather than preferential tax treatment). In addition, the introduction in the United States of a value-added tax, and an increase in currently very low VAT rates in Japan (as part of the ongoing reform of taxation), could yield significant resources while minimizing distortions associated with other types of tax increases.

The history of failed consolidation attempts also points to the importance of strong fiscal institutions. Good institutions—accurate and timely monitoring of fiscal outturns, coordination across levels of government, and fiscal rules—can play a critical role in preventing spending overruns or drawing attention to them in time for offsetting measures to be introduced. More is needed in this area, including in the largest advanced economies. Both Japan and the United States should underpin their fiscal consolidation efforts with institutional reforms. In the United States, more binding multiyear restrictions on spending are needed, along with effective top-down budgeting that helps ensure that plans are implemented. For Japan, the new medium-term fiscal framework needs to spell out the measures that will be taken. Greater commitment could also derive from breaking with the past practice of repeated recourse to supplementary budgets, except in emergency circumstances like those prevailing in the aftermath of the earthquake. In all countries, ensuring fiscal transparency is critical to maintaining credibility.

Tackling long-term spending pressures in advanced economies requires deep entitlement reforms, which should not be postponed further. The major spending pressures and policy challenges relate to health care; policymakers will have to balance the need to ensure access with the requirement of preserving sustainability of public finances. The most-promising reforms combine top-down budget control with bottom-up reforms to improve efficiency. In emerging economies, the main challenge will be to improve health safety nets while preserving long-term fiscal sustainability, as health indicators are substantially lower than in advanced countries. By contrast, pension spending pressures look more manageable, thanks to reforms already enacted. However, relatively optimistic baseline assumptions in some countries, including those regarding productivity growth, imply risks. In addition, several countries, including some emerging European economies (e.g., the Russian Federation and Ukraine), face rapid demographic changes and still need to conduct important reforms.

For advanced and emerging economies facing funding pressures and high debt levels, public debt management needs to be strengthened further. Efforts to lengthen maturities and smooth redemption profiles need to proceed, and strategies need to be developed that consider a diversified investor base, with a view to mitigating rollover risks.

Finally, building public support for large adjustment efforts will be key. The analysis of past consolidation attempts reveals that public support, rather than the presence of a strong legislative majority, was a major determinant of successful fiscal adjustments. Thus, a priority going forward should be to better explain to the public the rationale for and scale of the needed fiscal measures. Just as critically, it will be essential to ensure that the burdens of adjustment, as well as the benefits of the recovery, are distributed equitably across society. In this context, ensuring adequate social safety nets to protect the most vulnerable is of the utmost importance.

1 Tackling the Challenge of Health Care Reform in Advanced Economies

This appendix (drawing from IMF, 2010a) discusses approaches to contain "excess cost growth": the rise in public health spending over GDP in excess of what is due to population aging.

The Potential Impact of Health Reforms in Advanced Economies

Econometric analysis suggests that several policy options are available to help contain the growth of public health spending. The analysis presented here uses recently compiled Organization for Economic Cooperation and Development (OECD) data (Joumard, Andre, and Nicq, 2010) on key characteristics of health care systems (such as the extent of private health care provision, degree of regulation, availability of patient choice, and stringency of budget constraints) to evaluate the relationship between indices of these characteristics and the growth of public health spending. The impact of particular reforms on the growth rate of public health expenditure is then simulated by looking at the impact of hypothetical changes to a country's rating on these indices. Table A1.1 shows the estimated impact on excess cost growth (ECG) of a country's moving up one unit in any given OECD index, keeping all other indices fixed. The results suggest that substantial reductions in ECG could be obtained through extending market mechanisms (–0.50), improving public sector management and coordination (–0.30), and strengthening budget caps (–0.24). This compares with the average ECG, based on IMF staff econometric work, of about 1.0, which is incorporated into the staff's baseline projections.

Health care reforms could help slow the growth of spending in this area over the next 20 years. Figure A1.1 shows the average impact of reforms on public health spending-to-GDP ratios in 2030, grouped in five categories: budget caps (including budget constraints and central government oversight), public management and coordination (including "gatekeeping" processes that require referrals for accessing specialized care and subnational government involvement), market mechanisms (including choice of insurers and providers, private provision, and the ability of insurers to compete), demand-side reforms (including expansion of private insurance and cost sharing), and supply controls (including regulation of the health care workforce). The figure shows the combined effect of raising countries to the OECD mean score on each of these indices, based on the impact of improvements reported in Table A1.1.[22]

The results suggest that reforms of market mechanisms can be powerful, yielding a reduction in spending of about ½ percentage point of GDP. The exercise also underscores the importance of budget caps, which can reduce spending by ¼ percentage point of GDP. The simulated impacts of demand-side reforms and supply constraints are small, but not negligible. The variation in the impact on spending across categories, as shown in the figure, largely reflects differences in the size of the impact coefficients in Table A1.1, rather than substantial differences in the dispersion of index scores across categories.

---

[22] For the United States, which was not included in the OECD study of health institutions, the simulations show only the impact of an increase in the indices for strengthening of budget caps and supply controls. For this exercise, the value of the budget caps and supply controls indices for the United States is set equal to the average for the bottom 50 percent of the distribution on each of these indices.

Table A1.1. Relationship between Key Characteristics of Health Care Systems and Excess Cost Growth

Reform Areas and Indices	Impact of a One-Unit Change in Index on Excess Cost Growth [1]
Market Mechanisms	**-0.50**
Of which:	
Choice of insurers : Ability of people to choose their insurer for basic coverage	-0.22
Insurer levers : Ability of insurers to compete and availability of insurer information for consumers	-0.17
User information : Availability of information on quality and prices of health care services	0.11
Private provision : Degree of private provision of physician and hospital services	-0.14
Choice among providers : Degree of freedom in choosing among primary care physicians, specialists, and hospitals	-0.08
Public Management and Coordination	**-0.30**
Of which:	
Gatekeeping : Obligation or incentive to register with a general practitioner and/or to get referrals to access secondary care	-0.04
Subnational government involvement : Number of key decisions taken at the subnational level	-0.36
Delegation : Number of key decisions taken at the insurer level	0.10
Budget Caps	**-0.24**
Of which:	
Budget constraint : Rules and/or targets to fix the health budget and its allocation across subsectors and/or regions	-0.03
Central government oversight : Number of key decisions overseen by central government	-0.22
Demand-Side Reforms	**-0.09**
Of which:	
Over-the-basic coverage : Share of the population covered by nonprimary insurance, share of health care expenditures financed out of private insurance and degree of market concentration	-0.10
Price signals on users : Extent to which patients face out-of-pocket expenses	0.01
Supply Controls	**-0.06**
Of which:	
Regulation of workforce and equipment : Degree of regulation on the number and distribution of health care workforce and hospital high-tech equipment and activities, and control of recruitment and remuneration of hospital staff	-0.05
Priority setting : Definition of health benefit basket, effective use of health technology assessment, and definition and monitoring of public health objectives	-0.01
Contracting Methods	**0.09**
Of which:	
Volume incentives : Degree of payment modes to incentivize fewer services	0.09
Price Controls	**0.11**
Of which:	
Regulation of providers' prices : Regulation of drug prices and of prices billed by physicians and hospitals	0.05
Regulation of prices paid by third-party payers : Regulation of prices paid by third-party payers for primary care physicians, specialists, hospital services, and drugs	0.06

Sources: Joumard, Andre, and Nicq (2010); and IMF staff estimates.

[1] Impact on excess cost growth of public health spending due to one-unit change in each OECD index. OECD indices have been mapped to reform categories, although some overlap remains. In simulating the potential impacts of further reforms, only reforms that the econometric analysis shows to be effective in reducing excess cost growth are included.

Figure A1.1. Average Impact of Reform Components on Health Spending, 2030

(Decrease relative to the baseline; percent of GDP)

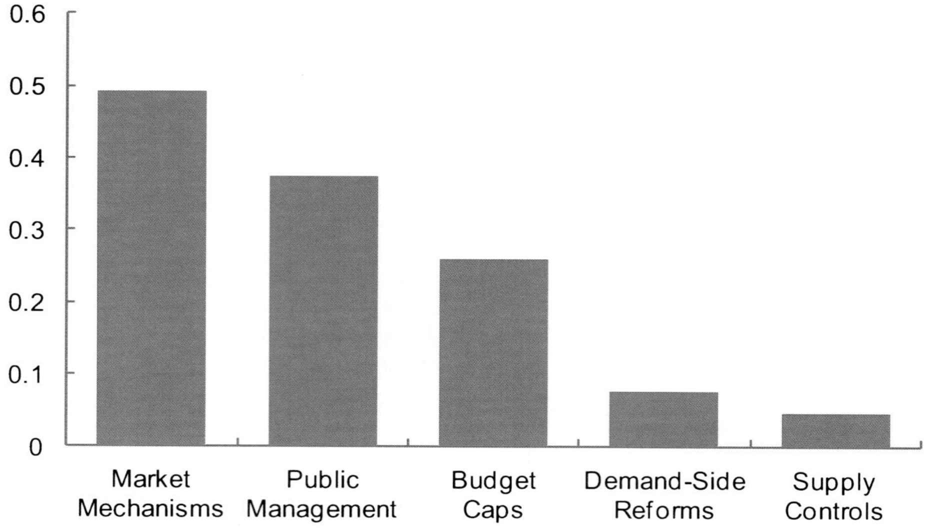

Sources: OECD Health Database; and IMF staff estimates.
Note: Unweighted averages of the impact of reforms.

It is important to note that the possible savings under reforms are subject to uncertainty. Simultaneous reforms across different aspects of the health system may be undesirable or counterproductive. Thus, the effect of the reforms across categories depicted in Figure A1.1 cannot necessarily be aggregated. Some reforms, however, could be complementary, implying that the savings under any particular reform may be understated.

The impact of the simulated reforms might still fall short of what would be needed in some countries to stabilize public health care spending-to-GDP ratios at current levels. Thus, additional efforts would be needed to achieve this target, or fiscal adjustment might need to rely more on cuts in other areas or additional revenue increases.

- This is especially important in some advanced European economies with relatively high projected growth in public health spending, such as Austria, Portugal, Switzerland, and the United Kingdom.

- In the United States, the challenge would be even larger. The illustrative savings from an assumed increase to the mean in the category of budget caps would yield savings of about 1 percentage point of GDP. Other options to reduce spending, beyond those captured in the econometric analysis, include the extension of health information technology, which would yield savings of ¼ percent of GDP.[23] Curtailing the favorable tax treatment of health insurance contributions (which involve tax expenditures—see Appendix 5—amounting to about 2 percent of GDP) could potentially yield large savings, and recent proposals in this area would yield savings of an additional ½ percentage point of GDP on an annual basis.[24] All told, these reforms, including those simulated in the econometric analysis, would reduce spending (including tax expenditures) by about 2 percentage points of GDP. Even with the reforms, however, health spending would still be rising by 3 percentage points of GDP.

Reform options and the appropriate mix of reforms will depend on country characteristics and the projected outlook for the growth of public health spending. The reform impacts simulated above focus on strengthening cost-containing characteristics of health systems on which countries score below the OECD mean. Of course, all of the identified reforms using this methodology may not necessarily apply to every country. Nevertheless, this approach provides a systematic way to identify potential reforms. Box A1.1 provides an assessment of options using this approach.

Health reform proposals raise two important questions. First, will cost-reducing reforms adversely affect health outcomes? Second, will reforms imply a fundamental change in the role of the state in the provision of health care services?

---

[23]See Hillestad and others (2005) and U.S. Congressional Budget Office (2008).

[24]See U.S. Senate Joint Committee on Taxation (2008). A recent proposal to replace the employer-sponsored health insurance tax exclusion in the United States with a credit indexed to the consumer price index would save, it is estimated, a little over 5 percent of GDP cumulatively over the next 10 years (Committee for a Responsible Federal Budget, 2010).

- The relationship between cost containment and the provision of high-quality health services varies by reform (Brereton and Vasoodaven, 2010; Cutler, 2004; Or and Hakkinen, 2010). Most micro-level efficiency reforms, such as the introduction of competition, can improve the responsiveness of the health system to patients but also reduce the growth of spending. It is thus possible, with an appropriate mix of reforms, to control spending without adversely affecting outcomes.

- Reforms have implications for the range of services or products financed by the public sector. As part of reforms to contain the growth of spending, countries may need to reduce the scope of the public benefits package. For predominately public sector systems, this could be achieved through greater reliance on cost sharing and private insurance. The expansion of the role of the private sector, however, needs to be accompanied by appropriate measures to ensure access, equity, and efficiency. Regulators also need to ensure adequate competition in the private insurance market.

Box A1.1. Potential Reform Strategies to Contain the Growth of Public Health Spending

Countries relying on market mechanisms

- In Canada, the Czech Republic, France, Germany, Japan, and the Slovak Republic, staying the course with marginal reforms would be enough to contain excess cost growth, although bolder reforms could still be needed to offset the effects of demographics on health spending.

- In Australia, Austria, Belgium, and the Netherlands, possible strategies include tightening budget constraints, strengthening gatekeeping (such as by requiring referrals to access secondary care), and increasing cost-sharing.

- Greece, Korea, Luxembourg, Switzerland, and the United States are projected to have relatively high spending growth, indicating the need for future reforms, especially for Greece and Luxembourg, which score low on efficiency measures.[1] These countries tend to have less stringent budget constraints, minimal central oversight (Korea and Luxembourg), lax regulations of the workforce and equipment, and little gatekeeping. Future efforts to contain spending growth in these countries should address these weaknesses.

Countries that rely more heavily on public insurance and provision

- Denmark and Ireland could focus on efficiency-enhancing reforms to reduce spending growth. Italy and Sweden, both of which score high in efficiency, could improve priority setting in the area of health (for example, by better monitoring public health objectives and the composition of the public health package).

- In Norway and Spain, containing the growth of spending could require tightening macro controls (including central oversight), broadening private insurance for care beyond the basic health package (Norway), and improving priority setting (Spain).

- Finland, Iceland, New Zealand, Portugal, and the United Kingdom have relatively high projected spending growth. Countries in this group could strengthen supply constraints on the workforce and equipment (for example, by rationing high-technology equipment). In addition, these countries could benefit from extending the role of private health insurance for over-the-basic care and increasing choice among providers (especially in Finland, New Zealand, and the United Kingdom).

Source: IMF (2010a).

[1]The assessment does not take into account reforms in Greece as part of its fiscal adjustment program initiated in 2010.

2 Fiscal Transparency Under Pressure

As governments seek to cut their debts and deficits in coming years, they may be tempted to supplement genuine fiscal adjustment with accounting stratagems. This happened during earlier episodes of adjustment, and there is evidence of a resurgence of the problem.[25] This appendix discusses some of these stratagems (drawing on examples mainly from Europe and the United States, where they have been documented most clearly) and suggests remedial actions.

Accounting Stratagems

In the short run, accounting stratagems typically increase reported revenue or decrease reported spending, but in return they decrease future revenue or increase future spending. Some stratagems are simple: with cash accounting and a lax definition of debt, governments can reduce deficits and leave reported debt unchanged, by deferring paydays and delaying payment of bills and tax refunds. Other stratagems, however, are more complex.

Most fiscal reporting standards do not recognize ordinary borrowing as revenue, but may treat similar, more complex transactions differently. For example:

---

[25] See, for example, Easterly (1999) and Koen and van den Noord (2005). Further references for the stratagems discussed here, including more recent ones, can be found in Irwin (2011) and, for the European examples, in the government finance statistics area of Eurostat's website (http://epp.eurostat.ec.europa.eu/portal/page/portal/government_finance_statistics/introduction).

- In a typical currency swap, two parties agree to make a series of payments to each other in different currencies but with equal expected present values. No money changes hands up front, and no debt is created. But if swap payments are based on an exchange rate other than the market rate, the two series of payments may have different present values and a debt may be created—but one that may not have to be reported as such. Greece, for example, used such swaps in 2001–07 to reduce reported debt by 2¼ percent of GDP at the end of 2009—until Eurostat scrutinized Greece's books.

- The Portuguese government recently assumed the pension assets and liabilities of Portugal Telecom, in a transaction that reduced the country's reported deficit for 2010 by 1½ percent of GDP. European reporting standards, set after a similar transaction by France in 1997, treat receipt of the assets as revenue without treating assumption of the obligations as spending. A comparable effect is achieved through the reversal of pension reforms, in which private second-pillar systems are returned to the public pay-as-you-go system (as in Argentina and Hungary): pension contributions provide an immediate boost to revenues, whereas the associated pension liability will translate into spending only in the future.

- The sale and lease-back of government property can disguise borrowing. For example, in the United States, the state of Arizona, in the face of restrictive constitutional limits on debt, raised $1 billion in 2010 through contracts in which the state sold various buildings and simultaneously leased them back.

Other stratagems defer the reporting of spending:

- In some public-private partnerships, the private sector invests in public buildings or infrastructure, and the government pays for services provided by the assets over the following decades. In the United Kingdom, obligations created by these arrangements amounted to some 2¼ percent of GDP in February 2010. In Portugal, such arrangements have created obligations worth about 3½ percent of GDP (not counting road contracts or contingent liabilities).[26]

- Another example of deferred spending relates to civil servants' pensions. Governments generally report the cash cost of paying pensions to retirees, but not the "employer contribution to pensions" element of their current employees' compensation package, since this does not require a cash outlay. In 2010, the U.S. federal government reported cash spending of $123 billion on military and civil service pensions in its deficit, whereas its less-publicized estimate of "net operating cost" in the government's financial statements counts the cost of the pensions at $312 billion.

Selling assets can reduce the deficit when the loss of the assets is not recognized:

- Many governments have privatized public enterprises to meet deficit targets, exploiting accounting standards that treated privatization receipts as revenue, but did not recognize the loss of future revenue associated with the transaction. Under other standards, such as those now used to calculate the deficit under Europe's excessive deficit procedure, the sale of shares of public enterprises does not reduce the deficit, but sales of nonfinancial assets, such as real estate, do. Of course, selling loss-making or barely profitable enterprises to owners that can improve their efficiency may improve the fiscal position of the government. But the reported fiscal improvement associated with selling profitable public enterprises can be much greater than the actual improvement.

- In the 2000s, many European governments securitized future revenues to reduce their reported deficits, selling rights to receive future revenues. Belgium and Portugal securitized tax receivables. Greece securitized

---

[26] The macroeconomic relevance of a public-private partnership program does not imply that it is solely motivated by an intent to defer spending, and countries such as Portugal and the United Kingdom assess the value for money offered by public-private partnerships and also disclose information on their future fiscal implications.

lottery proceeds, air traffic control fees, and EU grants. Italy reportedly raised €66 billion–€90 billion through securitizations.

Often governments reduce reported spending and debt by having it undertaken by entities excluded from fiscal accounts. In the United Kingdom, for example, when the privately owned rail network company failed, the government took over its liabilities, but designed the takeover in such a way as to ensure that the new company's liabilities did not count as government debt. At present, some of governments' biggest unrecognized debts relate to financial institutions. Eurostat concluded that Germany's banking crisis resolution entity should be classified as part of general government. It ruled, however, that Ireland had designed its entity as a private organization for accounting purposes, even though 95 percent of the costs would be funded with government-guaranteed debt. The U.S. federal government does not recognize as its own the liabilities (or assets) of Fannie Mae and Freddie Mac (see April 2011 GFSR).

The Size of the Problem

The nature of accounting stratagems means that reliable data on them are scarce, but the problem has clearly been substantial in some countries. By one measure (Koen and van den Noord, 2005), their average impact was more than 2 percent of GDP a year in Greece in 1993–2003, and roughly two-thirds of 1 percent in Italy and Portugal.

Further evidence of the significance of accounting choices for the measurement of fiscal aggregates comes from governments that publish relatively good fiscal information. The case of the United States is particularly useful because the federal government's fiscal decisions are influenced mostly by a mainly cash-based measure of the deficit, but the U.S. Treasury's annual *Financial Report of the U.S. Government* also includes a less-publicized accrual measure (net operating cost) that provides a better measure of long-run fiscal effects. In 1995–2010, the U.S. budget deficit underestimated long-run costs,

Table A2.1. Cash and Accrual Measures of the U.S. Federal Deficit

(Billions of U.S. dollars)

	2008	2009	2010
Budget Surplus	-455	-1417	-1294
Veterans' Compensation	-339	149	-224
Military and Civilian Employee	-211	-114	-279
Troubled Asset Relief Program	0	110	-86
Government-Sponsored Entities	0	0	-268
Other	-5	18	71
Net Operating Surplus	-1009	-1254	-2080

Source: U.S. Department of Treasury, Financial Management Service (2009, 2010).

as measured by net operating cost, by an average of 2 percent of GDP a year, mainly because the cash cost of veterans' compensation and civilian and military health and pension benefits was less than the accrued cost. Table A2.1 illustrates the difference between the two measures for 2008, 2009, and 2010.

Improving the Quality of Fiscal Reporting

Preventing the loss of fiscal transparency caused by accounting stratagems is difficult, but ensuring that governments report a balance sheet and several measures of the deficit can help. A suite of measures drawn from the *Government Finance Statistics Manual* (GFSM 2001) should include four measures of fiscal performance (cash balance [the sum of operating and investing cash flows], net operating balance, net lending, and change in net worth) and four measures of the fiscal position (gross debt, net debt, net worth of the general government, and public sector gross debt). It is helpful if governments also follow financial-reporting standards such as International Public Sector Accounting Standards (IPSAS), the development of which has drawn on experience with the use of accounting stratagems in the private sector. As well as being useful in its own right, such reporting can provide reliable data for fiscal statistics.

Long-term fiscal projections and statements of fiscal risk are also useful. Standard statistics and financial reporting can be supplemented by long-term fiscal projections, which reveal the long-run effects of current decisions, even when those effects are not picked up in measures of the deficit or debt. Statements of fiscal risk can be used to highlight contingent liabilities, although how such statements might deal with implicit liabilities is an unresolved problem.

The incentive to move fiscal operations to entities outside the government's accounts can be reduced by publishing statistics for the entire public sector, as well as financial reports prepared according to standards that require consolidation of entities controlled by government. Fiscal statistics in Europe and elsewhere focus on the general government, to the exclusion of public enterprises. There is good reason for using general government as the main unit of analysis, but an exclusive focus on the general government makes reporting too vulnerable to the shifting of spending and debts to other public entities. Reporting according to IPSAS is also helpful, because it requires governments to report as their own all activities of government-controlled entities, irrespective of legal status or function.

Lastly, more needs to be done to encourage compliance with standards. National audit institutions play a crucial role in ensuring the accuracy of financial reports by raising costs to government of publishing reports that do not comply with standards. Charters of budget honesty can help by requiring officials to certify the sincerity of budgets and financial reports. Independent statistical agencies and fiscal councils can help ensure that reporting is sheltered from political pressures. Media and nongovernmental organizations can help expose stratagems, and international financial institutions can provide independent surveillance: for example, with reports on compliance with fiscal standards, such as the IMF's code of fiscal transparency.

3

Assessing Fiscal Sustainability Risks: Deriving a Fiscal Sustainability Risk Map

Assessing a country's susceptibility to fiscal sustainability risks requires tracking a number of internal and external factors. The methodology elaborated in this appendix presents a framework to assess fiscal risks in a forward-looking manner along multiple dimensions based both on high- and low-frequency data and information. The results are presented in a Fiscal Sustainability Risk Map (Figure A3.1) that includes six dimensions: The first three refer to expected fiscal developments under the baseline scenario: short- and medium-term fiscal fundamentals (core fiscal indicators), long-term fiscal challenges, and asset and liability management. The other three dimensions refer to shocks that may affect the baseline arising from unexpected macroeconomic developments, financial sector problems, and policy implementation shortfalls or errors.[27]

The Six Dimensions of the Map

The indicators used to capture the six dimensions of the Fiscal Sustainability Risk Map are summarized below.

- *Core fiscal indicators.* They include the current year general government gross debt ratio (net debt for Australia, Canada, and Japan), the current

---

[27] See Cottarelli (2011) for a discussion of the overall approach. For more details see also Cheasty and others (2011) and Baldacci and others (2011).

year cyclically adjusted primary balance, and the projected growth-adjusted interest rate (five years ahead).

- *Long-term fiscal challenges.* Measures used to capture long-term fiscal challenges are the projected increases in pension and health care spending through 2050 compared to current year, the current year fertility rate, and the 20-year-ahead old-age-dependency ratio.

- *Liability structure.* This dimension includes gross financing needs, the share of short-term general government debt in total general government debt, the weighted average maturity of outstanding government debt, the ratio of short-term external debt to gross international reserves (for emerging economies only), the share of debt denominated in foreign currencies, and the share of general government debt held by nonresidents.

- *Macroeconomic uncertainty.* Near-term uncertainty is captured by the dispersion of one-year-ahead real GDP forecasts across analysts based on Consensus Forecasts. Medium-term uncertainty is assessed by the dispersion over time in countries' interest rate growth differential projections based on the semiannual WEO exercises.

- *Financial sector risks.* The indicators draw on the Global Financial Stability Map of the GFSR. For advanced economies, the GFSR's credit and market/liquidity risk index is used, complemented by a measure of contingent liabilities approximated by outstanding bonds of banks with government guarantees. For emerging economies, risks are captured by the GFSR's emerging market risk index.[28]

- *Policy implementation risk.* The risk measure is based on an assessment of the quality of countries' fiscal plans, using five criteria, and supporting budgetary institutions (based on the November 2010 *Fiscal Monitor* and Bornhorst and others, 2010).[29] Moreover, a measure of "government

---

[28] See Dattels and others. (2010) for a detailed discussion on the GFSR's Global Financial Stability Map.

[29] The criteria include whether medium-term fiscal goals have been specified, the level of commitment and specificity of policy measures in the fiscal plans, the composition of adjustment, and the degree to which measures to protect the most vulnerable are envisaged.

stability" enters, as captured by the corresponding component of the International Country Risk Guide risk indicator.

The indicators have been summarized using the following conventions. Indicators cover the G-20 advanced and emerging economies and some smaller advanced economies with large adjustment needs, with country group aggregations based on purchasing power parity GDP weights. Each dimension is an average (often weighted) of the subindicators and ranges from 0 to 10, with higher rankings signifying higher risks. A value of 5 should be interpreted as a broadly "neutral" outcome. In most cases, percentile rankings are used for each country compared to its historical values, with the historical average corresponding to the "neutral" level of 5. For the fiscal baseline variables, the normalization is not only over time but also compared to other countries; the related scores are combined with a fiscal stress index that assesses a country's susceptibility to extreme tail events. The index maps fiscal indicators into a summary score that depends on endogenous thresholds derived by minimizing the errors made in using each indicator to predict fiscal stress episodes (Baldacci and others, 2011).

Informed judgment enters into the final calibration of a country's position on the Fiscal Sustainability Risk Map. Staff judgment aims to account for the most recent information, which either may not yet be reflected in the data available or is difficult to capture quantitatively in the variables, and to reflect greater importance of certain risk factors at a given time.

Key Findings

Analysis of the indicators yields mixed results with regard to risks emanating from the baseline.[30]

- *Core fiscal indicators.* Risks stemming from short- and medium-term fiscal trends, as reflected in the core fiscal indicators, remain broadly unchanged across advanced economies, but are somewhat lower across

---

[30] While changes in the aggregate baseline indicators of less than 0.2 are considered in the text as "broadly stable," Figure A3.1 indicates the exact numerical changes over time.

emerging market economies. For the advanced economies, a worsening in the general government gross debt ratios and in the interest rate–growth differential is offset by a small improvement in cyclically adjusted primary balances (in 2011 compared to 2010).

- *Long-term fiscal challenges.* Risks from long-term fiscal challenges have remained broadly unchanged across both advanced and emerging market economies, reflecting limited reforms except most recently in France and Spain regarding pensions. All advanced economies continue to face significant risks due to spiraling health care costs.

- *Liability structure.* Rollover risks linked to the liability structure are also little changed in advanced economies, but have declined in emerging economies. For advanced economies, the broadly unchanged risk reflects an increase in financing needs, including in the United States, which has been offset by an improved debt structure. For emerging economies, smaller gross financing needs are projected for 2011, and higher reserves have helped lower the risk profile further.

With regard to shocks around the baseline, developments have diverged across advanced and emerging economies.

- *Macroeconomic uncertainty.* Near-term macroeconomic uncertainty has eased somewhat for advanced economies, but remains above its historical average. As activity has picked up in many advanced economies, the dispersion of real GDP forecasts for 2011 across analysts has narrowed markedly in recent months. This, however, does not yet reflect the amplified global downside risk stemming from higher-than-expected oil prices. In addition, there is somewhat greater volatility of medium-term projections regarding the interest rate growth differentials, reflecting increased uncertainty about the timing and strength of a potential shift from historically low interest rates. For emerging economies, macroeconomic uncertainty is still below that of advanced economies but has increased compared to six months ago. While the one-year-ahead real GDP growth dispersion indicator has fallen in recent months, overheating and inflationary pressures in some economies and rising food and commodity prices, as well as the uncertainties associated with the political turmoil in some countries in North Africa and the Middle East, have increased as risk factors.

- *Financial sector risk.* This risk remains elevated in advanced economies, but has receded somewhat, reflecting favorable financial market performance. Contingent liabilities, when measured by bonds issued by banks with government guarantees, have remained broadly stable compared to November 2010 at around 6 percent of GDP, on average. In emerging economies, financial sector risk has stabilized at its historical average, while risk appetite has risen further.

- *Policy implementation risk.* In contrast to financial sector risk, policy implementation risk has increased somewhat since November 2010 in advanced economies, reflecting a weakening of existing policy frameworks in some economies, and greater political uncertainty about government stability and the ability to implement fiscal plans. The increase in risk due to these developments has been partially offset by a strengthening of fiscal plans and institutions in some countries.

Several additional factors have a bearing on fiscal sustainability risk, and although they are not explicitly incorporated here, they are reflected in various parts of the risk map. For example, market sentiment or risk appetite affects governments' ability to raise funding and the price at which they can do so. Until the earthquake and ensuing events in Japan, and the political turmoil in the Middle East, market sentiment had improved significantly in advanced economies and risk appetite for emerging market assets had increased. Over the past weeks, however, the sentiment has weakened somewhat, and the indicator for implied volatility of equity markets, which peaked temporarily in the autumn of 2010, has increased again. Market sentiment is in part reflected in the financial sector risk assessment. Nonfiscal imbalances, such as current account imbalances or large private sector balance sheet exposures, can also heighten fiscal risks and are reflected in macroeconomic uncertainty and financial sector risks (Cottarelli, 2011).

Figure A3.1. The Fiscal Sustainability Risk Map

a. Advanced Economies

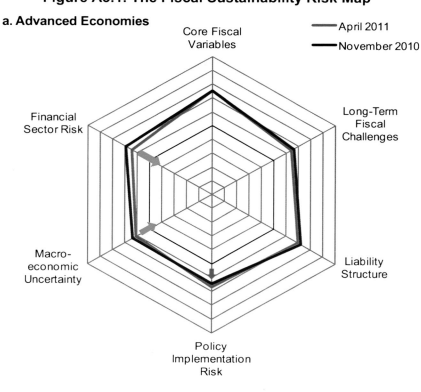

b. Emerging Economies

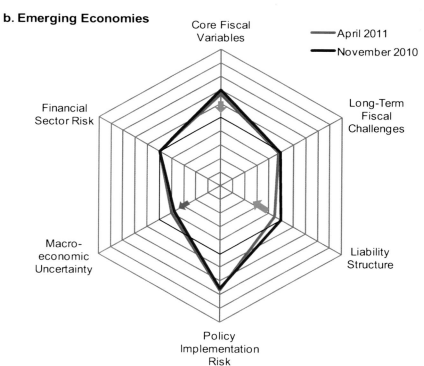

Source: IMF staff estimates.

Note: Greater distance from center indicates higher risk.

In sum, the indicator-based approach and the Fiscal Sustainability Risk Map signal that the fiscal sustainability risk is high in advanced economies, while it is generally lower for emerging economies, although new risk factors have emerged for the latter.

4 What Failed and What Worked in Past Attempts at Fiscal Adjustment

A systematic and comprehensive analysis of past adjustment plans and their outcomes provides useful insights for fiscal consolidation going forward: although today's circumstances may differ from those in the past, history offers lessons regarding pitfalls to avoid and successes to be replicated.[31] This appendix summarizes the main findings of individual country case studies and a cross-country statistical analysis, and puts forward some implications for the design and implementation of current fiscal adjustment plans.

Analytical Framework

Previous empirical studies have typically identified fiscal adjustment episodes on the basis of ex post outcomes: that is, the largest observed improvements in government debt or fiscal balance.[32] This appendix identifies fiscal adjustment *plans* on the basis of large *envisaged* reductions in debts and deficits. It thus goes beyond past successes, focusing also on attempts that eventually failed. The analysis tracks ex post outcomes compared with ex ante plans, looking at deviations from targets in revenues or expenditures and the factors underlying such deviations.

Case studies focus on each of the G-7 countries. Specific ex ante consolidation attempts in those countries have been selected based on the

---

[31] This appendix summarizes work undertaken by IMF staff and coauthors in Mauro (2011).

[32] See, for example, Alesina and Perotti (1995), Alesina and Ardagna (2009), and Giavazzi, Jappelli, and Pagano (2000).

size of the planned adjustment, formal and public commitment to adjust, detailed formulation, and medium-term perspective. Table A4.1 summarizes the plans analyzed and their main features. The case studies are complemented by a cross-country statistical analysis drawing on the three-year Convergence or Stability and Growth Programs produced by European Union countries during 1991–2007 (covering 66 plans that envisaged a general government balance improvement of at least 1 percent of GDP cumulatively over the three-year period).

Key Findings

The analysis yields findings in three dimensions: rationale for and design of the envisaged fiscal adjustment, degree of implementation and underlying macroeconomic factors, and political and institutional determinants of the implementation record.

Rationale for and design of fiscal adjustment plans

Rationale. Adjustments in the 1970s and early 1980s focused on fiscal deficits to tackle macroeconomic imbalances, such as rising inflation and external current account deficits (e.g., France, Germany, and the United Kingdom). Since the mid-1980s, plans have usually been introduced in response to high or rising public debt. Refinancing concerns have not been a major factor in these countries, but in some cases (e.g., Canada in the 1990s, Italy in the run-up to European Monetary Union, EMU) rising interest costs and spreads relative to neighboring countries were a motivating factor. In Europe, an enhanced focus on fiscal adjustment was driven by the Maastricht criteria, the Stability and Growth Pacts, and the excessive deficit procedure.

Envisaged composition of fiscal adjustment. Most plans focused on spending cuts, consistent with the relatively large initial size of government, particularly in Europe. Indeed, only 10 out of the 66 plans in the EU sample envisaged increases in the revenue-to-GDP ratio backed up by revenue measures. Furthermore, several plans called for a reduction in this ratio, requiring expenditure cuts larger than the targeted deficit reduction.

Table A4.1. Main Features of Selected G-7 Fiscal Adjustment Plans

Country	Adjustment Plan	Objectives / Design	Comments / Outcome
Canada	1985–91	• Reduce overall deficit by 3½ percent of GDP over six years. • Across-the-board cuts and freezes.	Overall deficit objectives met, but not sufficiently ambitious to halt the rise in debt.
	1994–97	• Reduce overall deficit by 3 percent of GDP over three years. • Major restructuring of spending, including reforms of unemployment insurance, transfers to provinces, and pensions.	Successfully met objectives and attained long-lasting reversal of debt dynamics.
France	Plan Barre, 1976–77 Virage de la Rigueur, 1982–84	• Austerity packages to curb inflation and current account deficit. • Not set in multiyear frameworks. • Combination of tax hikes and spending curbs. • Reforms in 1982–84.	Effective in reducing deficits and containing aggregate demand, but impact short-lived.
	1994–97 Plan aimed at meeting the Maastricht criteria	• Introduced multiyear framework. • Quantitative objectives aimed at meeting Maastricht criteria.	Met Maastricht criteria, partly through last-minute revenue measures. Difficulties in controlling expenditures.
	2003–07 Consolidation under the excessive deficit procedure	• Fiscal adjustment focused on expenditure control; revenue-to-GDP ratios targeted to remain stable. • Legally binding zero real growth rule for central government spending. • Health and pension reforms.	Some expenditure slippages, partly offset by one-off revenues.
Germany	1976–79 Plan	• Cut deficit by 2¾ percent of GDP. • Back-loaded; focus on expenditures (generalized cuts; cuts in labor market expenditures; wage restraint).	Weak economic growth led government priority to shift from fiscal adjustment to stimulus.
	1981–85 Plan	• Cut deficit by 1¼ percent of GDP. • Front-loaded expenditure cuts (reduction in entitlement and wage bills).	Largely successful.
	1991–95 Plan	• Cut deficit by 1½ percent of GDP while minimizing tax increases needed to finance unification. • Mainly expenditure-based (defense, social spending); revenue package from 1990 plus VAT rate hike.	Did not meet objectives.
	2003–07 Plan	• Cut deficit together with "Agenda 2010" structural reforms (labor market, pensions). • Back-loaded. All on expenditure side: reducing unemployment insurance, transfers to pension system, firing benefits, and subsidies.	Largely successful. Higher-than-expected costs of labor market reforms. Increase in VAT made it possible to meet objectives while reducing the tax burden on labor.
Italy	1994 Economic and Financial Program Document (EFPD) for 1994–97	• Reduce the debt-to-GDP ratio beginning in 1996. • Strong interest in joining EMU. Initial plan did not aim at meeting Maastricht criterion of 3 percent deficit, but objectives made more ambitious in midcourse.	Attained lasting reduction in debt-to-GDP ratio, albeit at high levels. Maastricht criterion met through last-minute efforts.
	2002 EFPD for 2002–05	• Planned limited improvement in fiscal balance (by 1 percent of GDP), together with a 2 percent of GDP reduction in the revenue ratio, thus implying the need for a 3 percent of GDP expenditure cut.	Revenue ratio remained unchanged. Large expenditure and fiscal balance overruns.

Table A4.1. Main Features of Selected G-7 Fiscal Adjustment Plans

(concluded)

Country	Adjustment Plan	Objectives / Design	Comments / Outcome
Japan	1997–Fiscal Structural Reform Act	• Reduce deficit to 3 percent of GDP by FY2003. • No revenue-enhancing measures announced. Future policy decisions needed to achieve targets.	Immediately derailed by Asian crisis and domestic banking crisis.
	2002–Medium-Term Fiscal Adjustment Plans. (Two subperiods: 2002– and 2006–).	• Aim for primary surplus by early 2010s. • Introduced 5-year frameworks. • Three-year expenditure ceilings on initial budgets by major policy area introduced in FY2006. • No revenue-enhancing measures announced. Future policy decisions needed to achieve targets.	Partially successful in the initial stages. Ultimately derailed by the global crisis.
United Kingdom	Howe's 1980 Medium-Term Financial Strategy (FY1980–83)	• Curb government borrowing to rein in the money supply and inflation. • Envisaged 5½ percent of GDP cut in the deficit, through lower spending and an expected rise in oil revenues.	Expenditure overruns in social security, public wages, and support to public enterprises.
	Lawson's 1984 Budget (FY1984–88)	• Rebalance the tax burden from direct to indirect taxes and reduce marginal tax rates. • Shrink the state (Thatcher government agenda). • Reduction in public sector manpower.	Expenditure cuts beyond what was envisaged. Privatization of large public enterprises.
	Clarke's November 1993 Budget (FY1994–98)	• Eliminate the 8 percent of GDP deficit by 1998. • Increases in national insurance contribution rate and excises, broadening of the VAT base. Freezes on running costs combined with zero-based budgeting "fundamental expenditure reviews."	Delivered a steady reduction in the fiscal deficit.
	Darling's 2007 Pre-Budget Report and Comprehensive Spending Review (FY2008–12)	• Planned modest reduction in the deficit, by reducing the growth of spending.	Derailed by global crisis: revenue underperformance, expenditure overruns, capital injections into banks.
United States	1985 Gramm-Rudman-Hollings (GRH) (Balanced Budget and Emergency Deficit Control Act)	• President to submit budgets consistent with GRH targets each year and balanced budget by 1991. • If legislated policy was projected to result in higher deficits, automatic "sequestration" with spending cuts would apply.	Did not achieve targets but deficit would have been larger in absence of GRH.
	OBRA–1990 (Omnibus Budget Reconciliation Act)	• Reduce deficit by cumulative US$500 billion (equivalent to 8.5 percent of 1991 GDP) in 1991–95. • Introduced discretionary spending caps and pay-as-you-go (PAYGO) mechanism. Included some tax increases.	Unable to restrain the unexpected growth in spending for entitlement programs (notably, Medicare and Medicaid).
	OBRA–1993	• Reduce the deficit by 1988 by 1¾ percent of GDP, relative to the no-policy-change baseline. • PAYGO continued and discretionary spending caps extended, with five-year nominal spending freeze. Some tax increases and measures to close loopholes.	Deficit reduction well in excess of targets, with stronger-than-expected economic growth and revenues, but also effective spending caps.

Source: IMF staff compilations.

Macroeconomic assumptions. Macroeconomic assumptions were mostly in line with those of independent observers (such as *Consensus Forecasts* and the IMF's *World Economic Outlook*). In other words, any surprises in economic growth (see below) and other macroeconomic variables were largely surprises for all observers.

Implementation record and underlying macroeconomic factors

Implementation record and degree of ambition. For the 66 plans in the EU sample, the average annual planned improvement in the structural fiscal balance was equivalent to 1.7 percent of GDP (cumulative over the three years), whereas the outturn was a 0.9 percent improvement. On a positive note, actual implementation was not weakened by greater ambition: higher planned adjustment was associated with higher actual adjustment by a factor of one (observations are scattered closely around the 45-degree line in Figure A4.1). This evidence suggests that it is "OK to plan big" because ambitious plans tend to produce more adjustment than do more modest ones.

Revenue-expenditure mix in outcomes versus plans. In most of the case studies, expenditure cuts did not materialize to the extent initially envisaged; by contrast, revenues often turned out to be above expectations, because of favorable cyclical developments in macroeconomic or asset price conditions and/or the introduction of (temporary) revenue measures to offset difficulties in implementing expenditure cuts. The cross-country statistical evidence confirms these findings: while plans envisaged cuts in the ratio of structural primary spending to potential GDP of 1.8 percent on average, actual cuts amounted to 0.3 percent. In contrast, revenues overperformed, partially offsetting the expenditure overruns (Table A4.2).

Role of economic growth. Deviations of economic growth from initial expectations were a key factor underlying success or failure. Some adjustment plans (e.g., Germany in the 1970s, Japan) were derailed, almost immediately, by unexpected economic downturns. Lower growth had a direct negative impact on cyclical revenues (and, to a lesser extent, caused an increase in some expenditure items), thereby worsening the headline fiscal balance. In addition, it had an indirect impact by tilting the authorities'

Figure A4.1. European Union: Planned and Actual Adjustments, 1991–2007

(Percent of potential GDP)

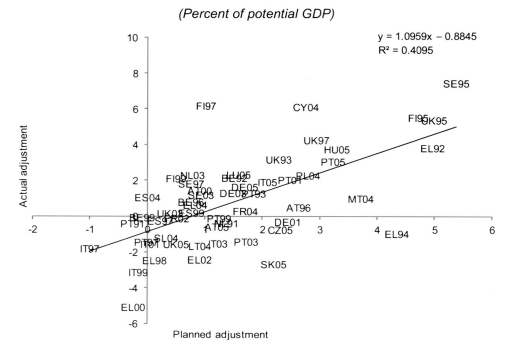

Source: EU countries' convergence plans and stability and growth plans; European Commission's Annual Macroeconomic Database (AMECO); and IMF staff estimates.

Note: Austria (AT), Belgium (BE), Cyprus (CY), Czech Republic (CZ), Finland (FI), France (FR), Germany (DE), Greece (EL), Hungary (HU), Italy (IT), Lithuania (LT), Luxembourg (LU), Malta (MT), Netherlands (NL), Portugal (PT), Slovak Republic (SK), Slovenia (SL), Sweden (SE), United Kingdom (UK). The two-digit numbers indicate the year when the plan was drawn up.

perception of the relative merits of fiscal consolidation versus fiscal stimulus. Conversely, the success of some plans (e.g., in the United States in the 1990s) was facilitated by higher-than-expected growth and asset price developments. In the cross-country analysis, a 1 percentage point improvement in growth compared with expectations resulted, on average, in a ½ percent of GDP strengthening in the headline fiscal balance.

Structural reforms. The case studies reveal that fiscal adjustment plans were more likely to meet their objectives when they were grounded in structural reforms. This was evident in Germany in the 1980s and 2000s, with structural reforms to the social welfare system; in the United Kingdom with the "Lawson adjustment" of the 1980s, which curbed expenditures as part of Prime Minister Margaret Thatcher's redefinition of the role of the state; and

Table A4.2. Actual versus Planned Structural Fiscal Adjustment, G-7

(Percent of potential GDP)

	∆PLAN	∆ACTUAL	Error = ∆ACTUAL minus ∆PLAN (0 is perfect implementation)	Median Implementation Ratio = ∆ACTUAL/∆PLAN (1 is perfect implementation)
Revenues	0.1	1.0	0.9	0.5
Cyclical	0.2	0.5	0.3	1.2
Structural	-0.1	0.5	0.6	...
Expenditures	-2.3	-1.0	1.3	0.4
Primary	-1.8	-0.3	1.5	0.2
Interest	-0.5	-0.6	-0.1	1.0
Structural Primary Balance	1.7	0.9	-0.8	0.8

Sources: "Convergence" and "Stability and Growth" programs (plans); European Commission's AMECO database (outturns).

Note: ∆PLAN and ∆ACTUAL refer to the planned and actual *change* in each item, in percent of potential GDP. Statistics reported are means, with the exception of those in the final column, which are medians.

in Canada in the 1990s, in the context of a repositioning of the role of the state supported by a comprehensive expenditure review. In contrast, plans in the same countries that eschewed reforms failed to meet their targets.

Fiscal institutions and political factors

Features of fiscal institutions. Several aspects of fiscal institutions influenced the degree of implementation of fiscal adjustment plans:

- *Monitoring of fiscal outturns and policy response to data revisions.* Shortcomings in these areas were important in Italy, where a significant portion of the deviations of outturns from plans reflected upward revisions to the initial deficit and subsequent medium-term plans did not compensate for such revisions. In the cross-country analysis, upward revisions of deficits generally resulted in larger deficits at the end of the period, whereas downward revisions in the deficit were less likely to result in changes to the end-period deficit targets or outcomes.

- *Binding medium-term limits.* Although the presence of medium-term plans was one of the criteria for choosing the case studies reviewed, the extent to which the plans included binding limits on expenditures varied. As medium-term limits were made more legally binding, actual compliance with spending targets improved. This pattern was most noticeable in the United States (where constraints on discretionary expenditure allowed a more rapid improvement in the fiscal balance in the context of favorable growth and asset price developments), France, and the United Kingdom.

- *Contingency reserves.* Some plans used contingency reserves to build in space to cope with potential adverse shocks, accelerate the adjustment, or create room for reducing the tax burden in the event that no adverse shocks materialized. Contingency reserves played a role in the extent to which fiscal adjustment targets were met in the United Kingdom and, to a lesser extent, Canada.

- *Coordination across levels of government.* Although most adjustment plans were originally devised for the central government, several involved reductions in transfers to subnational governments or other public entities. The extent to which those entities undertook parallel fiscal consolidations was an important determinant of whether the general government balance improved (as in Canada) or challenges were encountered (France and the United Kingdom).

- *Fiscal rules.* The cross-country statistical analysis finds the intensity of national fiscal rules to be positively associated with the extent to which targets were met.

Political factors and public support for fiscal adjustment. The cross-country evidence yields mixed messages on the role of political factors: lower fractionalization in the legislative body (parliament, congress) and perceptions of greater political stability are to some extent associated with better implementation of plans; on the other hand, implementation of ambitious plans is not associated with more frequent changes in government. What emerges more clearly from the case studies, however, is the importance of public support. For example, opinion polls ahead of the mid-1990s consolidation in Canada showed broad public support for debt reduction. The authorities took advantage of this to put in place a communication strategy to reinforce support for their adjustment plan. In Germany, a general shift in the economic policymaking paradigm in the 1980s (against active short-term demand management) and a reformist platform of the left-of-center party in the 2000s helped sustain fiscal adjustment.

Implications for Planned Adjustments

These findings have a number of implications for the design and implementation of fiscal adjustment plans in the years ahead.

Embedding plans in frameworks that are resilient to shocks. Current fiscal adjustment plans do not sufficiently detail the envisaged policy response to shocks. As seen above, shocks, especially to economic growth, often derail fiscal adjustment. Plans thus need to explicitly incorporate mechanisms to deal with such shocks, permitting some flexibility while credibly preserving the medium-term consolidation objectives. Examples of helpful mechanisms include:

- *Multiyear spending limits.* To anchor the consolidation path, plans should include binding and well-defined ceilings for expenditures and their subcomponents, and would preferably be endorsed not just by the executive but also by the legislature. The ceilings could exclude items that are cyclical (e.g., unemployment benefits), nondiscretionary (e.g., interest payments), or fiscally neutral (e.g., EU-funded projects). Many of the current adjustment plans have been framed with multiyear frameworks, but only a few (e.g., Germany and the United Kingdom) include sufficiently detailed spending ceilings.

- *Cyclically adjusted targets* would let the automatic stabilizers operate in response to cyclical fluctuations. To ensure credibility, the methods used to adjust the fiscal variables for the cycle should be subject to outside scrutiny. Thus far, only the plans for Germany and the United Kingdom include cyclically adjusted targets.

- *Realistic/prudent macroeconomic assumptions* would reduce the risk of missing the fiscal targets. Using more conservative assumptions relative to independent observers could be justified in a context of high uncertainty, but should be relied on sparingly in order not to reduce credibility. In this respect, the November 2010 *Fiscal Monitor* notes that macroeconomic assumptions underlying some countries' current adjustment plans are more optimistic than other publicly available forecasts.

Monitoring and accountability. Implementation of plans should be supported by reliable and timely information. Targets need to be based on sound information on the initial state of public finances. Any revisions to the initial position should lead to fine-tuning the adjustment path while keeping the medium-term targets unchanged, if possible. Fiscal councils and peer-monitoring processes can enhance accountability in implementing adjustment plans.[33]

Composition of fiscal adjustment. The revenue-expenditure mix of fiscal consolidation plans needs to reflect country-specific societal preferences and structural fiscal characteristics. As reported in the November 2010 *Fiscal Monitor*, expenditure measures significantly outnumber revenue measures in current consolidation plans. This is consistent with the large size of the state in many advanced economies. Nevertheless, in light of the magnitude of needed adjustments and the implementation record of past plans, where revenue increases partly compensated for expenditure overruns, it would seem desirable to redouble monitoring efforts and enhance institutional mechanisms to ensure that expenditure ceilings are adhered to. It would likewise be prudent to prepare additional high-quality measures and reforms on the revenue side, to be deployed in the event of expenditure overruns.

Structural reforms. Structural reforms are needed to underpin successful implementation of large fiscal adjustment plans. Several current plans include measures to reduce the size of the public administration and the social welfare system, but few envisage tackling the thorniest sources of spending pressures: those from pension and, especially, health entitlements. Current plans would benefit from a greater emphasis on reforms in these areas.

---

[33] For example, in the European Union, the recently introduced European semester (a six-month period every year during which member states' policies will be reviewed to detect any inconsistencies and emerging imbalances) is expected to reinforce coordination while major budgetary decisions are still under preparation.

Building public support. Public support for fiscal adjustment, rather than a comfortable legislative majority, was a key determinant of successful fiscal adjustments. Thus, a priority going forward will be to build public support through communication campaigns. These would aim at educating the public about the scale of fiscal challenges, and explaining what can reasonably be achieved through reforms without overburdening taxpayers or unduly curtailing necessary public services.

5

Containing Tax Expenditures

Rolling back tax expenditures can make a critical contribution to meeting the needs for fiscal consolidation in many countries while also improving the efficiency and fairness of their overall fiscal systems. This appendix reviews the pros and cons, calculation, and magnitude of tax expenditures—and their control and elimination.

What Are Tax Expenditures?

Tax expenditures are government revenues foregone as a result of preferential tax treatment of specific sectors, activities, regions, or agents. Common forms are exemptions (exclusions from the tax base), allowances (deductions from the base), credits (deductions from liability), rate reliefs (reduction of the tax rate), and deferrals (postponing payment).

Tax expenditures have been used by countries to achieve diverse public goals:

- Increasing tax progressivity (such as reduced VAT rates for food and medicine)
- Encouraging investment, research, and savings (e.g., accelerated depreciation, tax credits for research and development [R&D], reduced rates on certain financial instruments or savings accounts)
- Stimulating the consumption of merit goods or items yielding social benefits beyond those enjoyed by the spender himself (e.g., deductions

for education and charitable gifts, R&D tax credits)

- Attracting investment, in particular, foreign direct investment, to certain sectors or regions (e.g., tax holidays for technology, mining, or tourism industries, free trade zones in poor and isolated regions).

Worthy as such objectives may be, tax expenditures have drawbacks that often make them inferior to spending measures (or doing nothing at all). Table A5.1 summarizes the main pros and cons, but a number of drawbacks stand out.

First, tax expenditures are often poorly targeted, which may lead to ineffectiveness. For example, poorer households may spend a larger share of their income on food than richer households, but since they spend a smaller absolute amount, they tend to receive less of the benefit from a reduced VAT rate: the poor would be better served by eliminating the rate reduction and protecting them through targeted spending measures. Allowances or deductions under the personal income tax help only those who fall into the tax net, effectively excluding many poor households, while corporate tax breaks are little use to companies (such as start-ups) with no taxable income. There are many other examples. Tax expenditures may not be well targeted to the activities they are intended to promote: mortgage interest relief, for instance, has commonly been justified as encouraging home ownership, but the evidence for the United States is that the effect has rather been to encourage owner-occupiers to buy larger properties. Likewise, R&D tax credits may promote R&D with large private rather than social returns.

Second, tax expenditures add to the complexity of the tax code and can be open to abuse: regional tax holidays and free zones, for instance, provide opportunities to reduce tax by transfer pricing profits out of profitable domestic enterprises in the rest of the country.

Third and not least, tax expenditures are less transparent than traditional forms of expenditure. Indeed, the very lack of transparency of tax expenditures sometimes accounts for their popularity with policymakers. They may escape the scrutiny applied to regular budgetary outlays and typically do not require annual renewal through the budget process.

Table A5.1. Comparison of Tax Expenditures and Direct Spending

	Tax Expenditures	Direct Spending
Accessibility for beneficiaries	Simple, because of their automatic nature.	More complex, requiring selection.
Administrative and compliance costs	High, if exemptions are properly monitored.	Medium, due to necessity of a selection and allocation system.
Possible abuses	Evasion, avoidance, and rent seeking.	Arbitrariness, inefficiency, and capture of the allocating body.
Flexibility	Work with permanent laws, thereby generating stability but also inertia.	Work with budgets, evaluations, and regular reallocations.
Transparency and accountability	Their automatic nature does not contemplate control mechanisms or accountability.	Must be approved by legislature, as with all governmental expenditure.
Expenditure control	Expenditure determined ex post; uncertain and unlimited, which can cause fiscal imbalances.	Programmed and controlled spending, limited by the budget law.
Equity	Only potential taxpayers benefit, and those with highest incomes often benefit the most.	Discretion can provide more equitable access, enhancing targeting of beneficiaries.

Source: Villela, Lemgruber, and Jorratt (2010).

Moreover, tax expenditures avoid increasing the overall level of government spending, which can be attractive to politicians worried about hostile public reaction to "big government."

This is not to say that tax expenditures are never worthwhile: a deduction for charitable gifts, for instance, may do a better job of allocating resources to activities that people want to support than would public spending, and in some cases, public spending may be more vulnerable to governance difficulties and abuse than are preferential tax arrangements. But both principle and experience suggest that tax expenditures should be regarded with skepticism.

How Big Are They?

Measuring tax expenditures is challenging. Key steps include

- Specifying some reference or "benchmark" tax system against which deviations or preferential treatments can be identified.[34]

- Estimating the fiscal costs, which can be interpreted and measured in different ways.[35]

- Constructing aggregate measures. This is especially tricky: in general, the complexities and nonlinearities in most tax systems mean that the revenue gain from eliminating tax expenditures A or B together is not the same as the sum of that from eliminating each of A and B in isolation. Aggregated tax expenditure numbers (like those presented below) must be treated with care.

Different methodologies and judgments as to what is or not considered a tax concession mean that tax expenditure budgets vary in size across countries more dramatically than do the underlying policies. For example, Chile uses a broader notion than other Latin American countries, so its tax expenditures look correspondingly large. Some countries choose to report a very limited list of tax expenditures, and cross-country comparisons can therefore be misleading (i.e., higher values do not always represent a larger amount of actual tax expenditures, but may arise instead from better and more comprehensive reporting).

---

[34]Alternatives are the *conceptual approach* (benchmark is some theoretically preferred tax structure), the *legal approach* (benchmark is the actual tax legislation framework that applies for activities not benefiting from preferential treatment), and the *analogous subsidy approach* (identifies as tax expenditures only those tax concessions analogous to a direct spending measure).

[35] There are three main methods: *foregone revenue* (revenue loss assuming that the concession does not change taxpayers' behavior), *earned revenue* (taking into account behavioral changes), and *equivalent direct expenditure* (the transfer that would leave taxpayers with an income similar to that which they obtain from the tax expenditure). Almost all countries use the foregone revenue method for its greater ease; only Sweden and the United States have tried equivalent direct expenditure as an additional method.

Figure A5.1. Tax Expenditures in 26 Countries
(Percent of GDP)

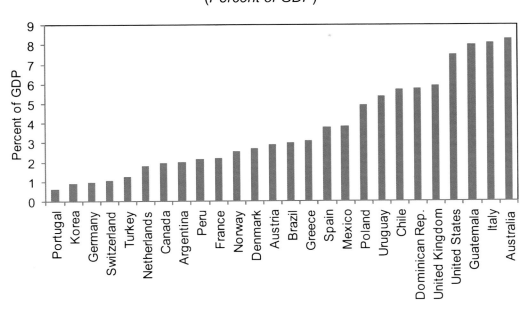

Sources: OECD (2010b); United States, National Commission on Fiscal Responsibility and Reform (2010); and websites of Latin American and Caribbean countries (Argentina, Brazil, Chile, Dominican Republic, Guatemala, Peru, and Uruguay).

Note: All estimates are for 2010, except that for Guatemala, which is for 2009.

Reliable numbers are in fact hard to find. However, OECD and Latin American countries generally offer good practices in measuring and reporting tax expenditures. Figure A5.1 shows, for 26 countries, the order of magnitude of total tax expenditures—subject to the caveats above. They vary from less than 1 percent of GDP to above 8 percent.[36] These numbers largely refer to the central government and could well be higher where subnational governments play a substantial role in revenue mobilization and are allowed to grant tax concessions (e.g., Brazil, the United States). The figures suggest that there is in many cases significant scope to raise additional revenue without increasing statutory tax rates. A particularly careful and powerful analysis of the scope for such reform was recently provided by the U.S. National Commission on Fiscal Responsibility and Reform (Box A5.1).

---

[36] To give just one example of the difficulty in comparing numbers, the VAT estimates for Portugal (which appears to have the lowest levels of tax expenditures in this set) include "exemptions" but not "reduced rates" (typically the largest VAT expenditure), whereas the estimates for other countries generally include both.

Box A5.1. The U.S. National Commission Report

A 2010 report issued by the U.S. National Commission on Fiscal Responsibility and Reform is highly critical of U.S. tax expenditures ("backdoor spending hidden in the tax code") with "corporations . . . able to minimize tax through various tax expenditures . . . as a result of successful lobbying." It estimates tax expenditures in the United States to be $1.1 trillion a year: about 7.5 percent of GDP.

The commission's recommendations are ambitious: instituting "zero-base budgeting" by eliminating all income tax expenditures and using the revenue to reduce rates and the deficit. Tax expenditures could then be added back only to support a small number of simpler and targeted provisions to promote work, home ownership, health care, charity, and savings.

If all tax expenditures were eliminated, the commission estimates, personal income tax rates could be reduced to as low as 8, 14, and 23 percent (from the 2011 progressive levels of 15, 28, 31, 36, and 39.6 percent), and the corporate income tax rate could be cut from 35 percent to 26 percent.

Can They Be Managed and Reduced?

The effective management of tax expenditures requires an adequate legal and institutional framework, supporting incentive mechanisms, and a systematic evaluation of costs and benefits.

Adequate legal and institutional framework

Managing tax expenditures is complex, given their multifunctional and intergovernmental nature. A clear legal framework is needed, as embodied in budgetary framework laws, fiscal responsibility laws, and/or tax codes. Tax expenditures should be granted only through tax or finance laws (not decrees, other infralegal instruments, or laws unrelated to taxation), and draft laws proposing new concessions should be accompanied by revenue loss estimates. It is good practice to estimate tax expenditures annually and to present a report alongside (or integrated with) the regular budgetary proposal to the legislature. Most OECD and Latin American countries do this, generally with detailed information by tax type. Some, like Brazil and Chile, perform additional analyses, including those regarding some regional and distributional impacts, respectively. Estimates are typically reported only for one year, but in some countries, such as Australia, Canada, the Netherlands, and the United States, the reports cover four or five years ahead.

Incentive mechanisms to control tax expenditures

Fiscal rules and other legal provisions can support the effective management of tax expenditures, limiting their increase—by sunset clauses, for instance, setting a deadline for the duration of tax expenditures or requiring evaluation after this period (e.g., those in Germany, Japan,[37] Korea, and Peru). Specific rules to cap the amount of tax expenditures in relation to tax revenues are very rare.[38] Nonbinding guidelines can also help control the expansion of tax expenditures, as with a 2006 Federal Cabinet guideline in Germany that new subsidies be given as grants, or "financial aids," not as tax expenditures.

Systematic evaluation of costs and benefits

Tax expenditures should be evaluated according to clear criteria, assessing their impact on public finances, economic efficiency, equity, and administrative and compliance costs—and on their likely effectiveness in reaching their underlying objective. For example, Germany has started a formal revision of its tax expenditures, starting with the largest 20 (accounting for 92 percent of total tax expenditures). The evaluation framework includes identifying macroeconomic motivations or perceived market failures; assessing effectiveness and efficiency, including impact on behavior,[39] and determining whether the tax expenditure is the best public policy instrument for pursuing the associated macro objective; and analyzing any side effects for the tax system.[40] The Netherlands has had a similar

---

[37] OECD (2010b) mentions that sunset clauses have functioned effectively in Japan, because they force tax officials and other related parties to review the contents of Special Tax Measures regularly.

[38] Korea seems to be the only OECD country that narrowly caps tax expenditures, through the adoption, in 2007, of a provision stating that the ratio of tax expenditures to the sum of tax expenditures and tax revenues should grow by at most 0.5 percent of its average over the previous three years (OECD, 2010b).

[39] For instance, a tax deduction for some item of spending increases aggregate private spending on it by more than the revenue foregone only if the elasticity of private spending with respect to unity minus the relevant marginal tax rate exceeds unity. More generally, Saez (2004) provides a framework for evaluating tax expenditures under the personal income tax aimed to encouraging spending on particular items.

[40] See OECD (2010b) for additional details.

commitment since 2004, with the objective of reviewing each tax expenditure every five years. Independent academic assessment also has an important role to play.

Ideally, a distinct administrative unit should be in charge of evaluation. The evaluation criteria should be clear and transparent, covering a number of factors: consistency with the macroeconomic framework; efficiency considerations; effectiveness in reaching intended goals, relative to alternatives; beneficiaries and impact on equity; and control of administrative and other costs (e.g., social, environmental, political).[41]

It Can Be Done

Reducing tax expenditures can mean taking on powerful interests. But it can be done. Some countries (the Slovak Republic, for instance) have done it by a wholesale reduction, so no one can complain of especially unfavorable treatment, perhaps sweetening the pill with some reduction of rates. In other cases they have been phased out, strategies for this including the conversion of deductions to credits calculated at the lowest marginal tax rate (or lower) and the fixing of caps in nominal terms: the United Kingdom has shown that, in this way, even mortgage interest relief can be removed.

---

[41] Administrative and compliance costs have not received much attention in evaluating tax expenditures. However, important costs arise from reporting and managing tax expenditures, such as the need for additional tax auditors to control tax concessions, the development of specific information systems, new tax forms or additional data requests from taxpayers, and specific intragovernmental procedures (e.g., between the tax administration and line ministries, or free zone regulators and customs authorities).

Methodological and Statistical Appendix

This appendix comprises four sections: assumptions, data and conventions, economy groupings, and statistical tables. The assumptions underlying the estimates and projections for 2011–16 are summarized in the first section. The second section provides a general description of the data and of the conventions used for calculating economy group composites. The classification of countries in the various groups presented in the *Fiscal Monitor* is summarized in the third section. The last section comprises the statistical tables on key fiscal variables. Data in these tables have been compiled on the basis of information available through early April 2011.

Fiscal Policy Assumptions

The historical data and projections of key fiscal aggregates are in line with those of the April 2011 WEO, unless highlighted. For underlying assumptions other than on fiscal policy, see the April 2011 WEO.

The short-term fiscal policy assumptions used in the WEO are based on officially announced budgets, adjusted for differences between the national authorities and the IMF staff regarding macroeconomic assumptions and projected fiscal outturns. The medium-term fiscal projections incorporate policy measures that are judged likely to be implemented. In cases in which the IMF staff has insufficient information to assess the authorities' budget intentions and prospects for policy implementation, an unchanged structural primary balance is assumed, unless indicated otherwise. The specific assumptions relating to selected economies follow.

Argentina. The 2011 projections are based on the 2010 outturn and IMF staff assumptions. For the outer years, the IMF staff assumes unchanged policies.

Australia. Fiscal projections are based on IMF staff projections and the 2010–11 Mid-Year Economic and Fiscal Outlook.

Austria. The historical figures and the projections for general government deficit and debt do not fully reflect the most recent revisions by Statistik Austria in the context of its fiscal notification to Eurostat.

Belgium. The data for 2010 are preliminary estimates by the National Bank of Belgium. IMF staff projections beyond 2011 are based on unchanged policies. The 2011 projections, however, include some of the planned measures for the 2011 federal budget still under preparation and the 2011 budgetary targets for the regions and communities, and the social security administration.

Brazil. The 2011 projections are based on the Budget Law and recent policy announcements that reduce the overall expenditure envelope by about 1.2 percent of GDP. Medium-term projections are based on unchanged policies and assume the authorities will maintain their commitment to a primary surplus of about 3 percent of GDP.

Canada. Projections use the baseline forecasts in the latest Budget 2011—A Low-Tax Plan for Jobs and Growth. The IMF staff has made some adjustments to this forecast for differences in macroeconomic projections. The IMF staff forecast also incorporates the most recent data releases from Finance Canada and Statistics Canada, including federal, provincial, and territorial budgetary outturns through the end of 2010.

China. For 2010–11, the government is assumed to continue and complete the stimulus program it announced in late 2008, although the lack of details published on this package complicates IMF staff analysis. Specifically, the IMF staff assumes the stimulus was not withdrawn in 2010, and so there is no significant fiscal impulse. Stimulus is withdrawn in 2011, resulting in a negative fiscal impulse of about 1 percent of GDP (reflecting both higher revenue and lower spending).

Denmark. Projections for 2010–11 are aligned with the latest official budget estimates and the underlying economic projections, adjusted where appropriate for the IMF staff's macroeconomic assumptions. For 2012–16, the projections incorporate key features of the medium-term fiscal plan as embodied in the authorities' 2009 convergence program submitted to the European Union.

France. For 2010, the general government data reflect the provisional outturn based on data released by the authorities on March 31, 2011. These data differ from the April 2011 WEO, where this update is not yet reflected. Projections for 2011 and beyond reflect the authorities' 2011–14 multiyear budget, adjusted for differences in assumptions on macro and financial variables, and revenue projections.

Germany. The estimates for 2010 are preliminary estimates from the Federal Statistical Office of Germany. The IMF staff's projections for 2011 and beyond reflect the authorities' adopted core federal government budget plan adjusted for the differences in the IMF staff's macroeconomic framework and staff assumptions on the fiscal developments in state and local governments, social insurance system, and special funds. The estimate of gross debt at end-2010 includes the transfer of liabilities of bad banks to the government balance sheet.

Greece. Macroeconomic and fiscal projections for 2010 and the medium term are consistent with the authorities' program supported by an IMF Stand-By Arrangement. Fiscal projections assume a strong front-loaded fiscal adjustment in 2010, followed by further measures in 2011–13. Growth is expected to bottom out in late 2010 and gradually rebound thereafter, coming into positive territory in 2012. The data include fiscal data revisions for 2006–09. These revisions rectify a number of shortfalls in earlier statistics. First, government-controlled enterprises in which sales cover less than 50 percent of production costs have been reclassified as part of the general government sector, in line with Eurostat guidelines. A total of 17 entities are affected, including a large number of loss-making entities. The debt of these entities ($7\frac{1}{4}$ percent of GDP) is now included in headline general government debt data, and their annual losses increase the annual deficit (to the extent their called guarantees were not reflected in previous deficit data). Second, the revisions reflect better information on arrears (including for tax refunds, lump sum payments to retiring civil service pensioners, and payments to health sector suppliers) and revised social security balances that reflect corrections for imputed interest payments, double-counting of revenues, and other inaccuracies. Finally, newly available information also helps explain the upward revision in debt data.

Hong Kong SAR. Projections are based on the authorities' medium-term fiscal projections.

Hungary. Fiscal projections are based on IMF staff projections of the macroeconomic framework, the impact of existing legislated measures, and fiscal policy plans as announced by end-December 2010.

India. Historical data are based on budgetary execution data. Projections are based on available information about the authorities' fiscal plans, with adjustments for the IMF staff's assumptions. Subnational data are incorporated with a lag of up to two years; general government data are thus finalized long after central government data. The IMF presentation differs from Indian national accounts data, particularly regarding divestment and license auction proceeds, net versus gross recording of revenues in certain minor categories, and some public sector lending.

Indonesia. The 2010 deficit was lower than expected (0.6 percent of GDP), reflecting underspending, particularly for public investment. The 2011 deficit is estimated at 1.5 percent of GDP, lower than the budget estimate of 1.8 percent of GDP. While higher oil prices will have a negative budgetary impact in the absence of fuel subsidy reform, this effect is likely to be offset by underspending, in particular on public investment, given significant budgeted increases. Fiscal projections for 2012–16 are built around key policy reforms needed to support economic growth, namely, enhancing budget implementation to ensure fiscal policy effectiveness, reducing energy subsidies through gradual administrative price increases, and continuous revenue mobilization efforts to increase space for infrastructure development.

Ireland. The fiscal projections are based on the 2011 Budget and the medium-term adjustment envisaged in the December 2010 EU/IMF-supported program. This includes €15 billion in consolidation measures over 2011–14, with €6 billion in savings programmed for 2011. The projections are adjusted for differences in macroeconomic projections between the IMF staff and the Irish authorities. The new government that assumed office in early March 2011 has also committed to the 2011–12 fiscal program and to further consolidation in the medium term.

Italy. The fiscal projections incorporate the impact of the 2010 budget law and fiscal adjustment measures for 2010–13, as approved by the government in May 2010 and modified during parliamentary approval in June–July. The 2010 budget balance data reflect the outturn based on data released by the Italian National Institute of Statistics on April 4, 2011. These data differ by 0.1 percent of GDP from the April 2011 WEO, where this update is not yet reflected. The IMF staff projections are based on the authorities' estimates of the policy scenario, including the above medium-term fiscal consolidation package and adjusted mainly for differences in the macroeconomic assumptions and for less optimistic assumptions concerning the impact of revenue administration measures (to combat tax evasion). After 2013, a constant structural primary balance (net of one-time items) is assumed.

Japan. The 2011 projections assume fiscal measures already announced by the government and reconstruction spending of around 1 percent of GDP. The medium-term projections typically assume that expenditure and revenue of the general government are adjusted in line with current underlying demographic and economic trends (excluding fiscal stimulus).

Korea. The fiscal projections assume that fiscal policies will be implemented in 2011 as announced by the government. The projection for for 2010 is mainly based on the outturn as of November 2010, assuming that the first 11 months had collected/used 92 percent of total revenue/expenditure. As a result, the fiscal impulse is projected to be –3 percent of GDP in 2010. Expenditure numbers for 2011 are broadly in line with the government's budget. Revenue projections reflect the IMF staff's macroeconomic assumptions, adjusted for the tax measures included in the multiyear stimulus package introduced in 2009 and discretionary revenue-raising measures included in the 2010 budget. The medium-term projections assume that the government will continue with its consolidation plans and balance the budget (excluding social security funds) by 2013.

Mexico. Fiscal projections are based on the IMF staff's macroeconomic projections; the modified balanced-budget rule under the Fiscal Responsibility Legislation, including the use of the exceptional clause; and the authorities' projections for spending, including for pensions and health care, and for wage restraint. For 2010–11, projections take into account departure from the balanced budget target under the exception clause of the fiscal framework, which allows for a small deficit reflecting a cyclical deterioration in revenues.

Netherlands. Fiscal projections for 2010–15 are based on the Bureau for Economic Policy Analysis budget projections, after adjusting for differences in macroeconomic assumptions. For 2016, the projection assumes that fiscal consolidation continues at the same pace as for 2015.

New Zealand. Fiscal projections are based on the authorities' 2010 budget and IMF staff estimates. The New Zealand fiscal accounts switched to generally accepted accounting principles beginning in fiscal year 2006/07, with no comparable historical data.

Portugal. 2010 data are preliminary. For 2011 and beyond, the IMF staff incorporates all approved fiscal measures (thus excluding the measures proposed in March 2011, but rejected by parliament). The fiscal numbers also incorporate the impact of the IMF staff's macroeconomic projections.

Russian Federation. Projections for 2011–13 are based on the non-oil deficit in percent of GDP implied by the draft medium-term budget and on the IMF staff's revenue projections. The IMF staff assumes an unchanged non-oil federal government balance in percent of GDP during 2013–16.

Saudi Arabia. The authorities adopt a conservative assumption for oil prices—the 2011 budget is based on a price of $54 a barrel—with the result that fiscal outcomes often differ significantly from the budget. IMF staff projections of oil revenues are based on WEO baseline oil prices discounted by 5 percent, reflecting the higher sulfur content in Saudi crude oil. Regarding non-oil revenues, customs receipts are assumed to grow in line with imports, investment income in line with the London interbank offered rate (LIBOR), and fees and charges as a function of non-oil GDP. On the expenditure side, wages are assumed to rise above the natural rate of increase, reflecting a salary increase of 15 percent distributed during 2008–10, and goods and services are projected to grow in line with inflation over the medium term. In 2010 and 2013, 13th-month pay is awarded based on the lunar calendar. Interest payments are projected to decline in line with the authorities' policy of repaying public debt. Capital spending in 2010 is projected to be about 32 percent higher than in the budget and in line with the authorities' announcement of $400 billion in spending over the medium term. The pace of spending is projected to slow over the medium term, leading to a tightening of the fiscal stance.

Singapore. For fiscal year 2011/12, projections are based on budget numbers. For the remainder of the projection period, the IMF staff assumes unchanged policies.

South Africa. Fiscal projections are based on the authorities' 2011 budget and policy intentions stated in the Budget Review, published February 23, 2011.

Spain. The 2010 numbers are the authorities' estimated outturns for the general government for the year. For 2011 and beyond, the projections are based on the 2011 budget and the authorities' medium-term plan, adjusted for the IMF staff's macroeconomic projections.

Sweden. Fiscal projections for 2010 are in line with the authorities' projections. The impact of cyclical developments on the fiscal accounts is calculated using the OECD's latest semielasticity estimates.

Switzerland. Projections for 2009–15 are based on IMF staff calculations, which incorporate measures to restore balance in the federal accounts and strengthen social security finances.

Turkey. Fiscal projections assume that the authorities adhere to their budget balance targets as set out in the 2011–13 Medium-Term Program. The cyclically adjusted balance refers to the general government and adjusts only for the standard output gap.

United Kingdom. Fiscal projections are based on the authorities' 2011 budget announced in March 2011, and the Office for Budget Responsibility's Economic and Fiscal Outlook published along with the budget. These projections incorporate the announced medium-term consolidation plans from 2011 onward. The projections are adjusted for differences in forecasts of macroeconomic and financial variables.

United States. Fiscal projections are based on the president's draft FY2012 budget adjusted for the staff assessment of policies likely to be adopted by Congress. Compared with the president's budget, the IMF staff assumes more front-loaded discretionary spending cuts, a further extension of emergency unemployment benefits, and a delayed action on the proposed revenue-raising measures. The IMF staff estimates of fiscal deficits also exclude certain measures yet to be specified by the authorities and are adjusted for a different accounting treatment of financial sector support. The resulting projections are adjusted to reflect the staff forecasts of key macroeconomic and financial variables and are converted to the general government basis.

Data and Conventions

Data and projections for key fiscal variables are based on the April 2011 WEO, unless indicated otherwise. Where the *Fiscal Monitor* includes additional fiscal data and projections not covered by the WEO, data sources are listed in the respective tables and figures. Unless otherwise indicated, all fiscal data refer to the general government where available and to calendar years, with the exceptions of Pakistan, Singapore, and Thailand, for which data refer to the fiscal year.

Composite data for country groups are weighted averages of individual country data, unless otherwise specified. Data are weighted by GDP valued at purchasing power parity (PPP) as a share of the group GDP in 2009. Fixed weights are assumed for all years, except in figures where annual weights are used.

For most countries, fiscal data follow the IMF's *Government Finance Statistics Manual 2001* (GFSM 2001). The concept of overall fiscal balance refers to net lending (+)/borrowing (−) of the general government. In some cases, however, the overall balance refers to total revenue and grants minus total expenditure and net lending.

Data on financial sector support measures are based on the IMF's Fiscal Affairs and Monetary and Capital Markets Departments' database on public interventions in the financial system, revised following a survey of the G-20 economies. Survey questionnaires were sent to all G-20 members in early December 2009 to review and update IMF staff estimates of financial sector support. This information was later completed using national sources and data provided by the authorities. For each type of support, data were compiled for the amounts actually utilized and recovered to date. The period covered is June 2007 to the latest available.

Statistical Tables 3 and 4 of this appendix present IMF staff estimates of the general government cyclically adjusted overall and primary balances. For some countries, the series reflect additional adjustments such as natural resource–related revenues or commodity-price developments (Chile, Peru), land revenue and investment income (Hong Kong SAR), tax policy changes and the effects of asset prices on revenues (Sweden), and extraordinary operations related to the banking sector (Switzerland). Data for Norway are for cyclically adjusted non-oil overall or primary balance.

Additional country information follows, including for cases in which reported fiscal aggregates in the *Monitor* differ from those reported in the WEO:

Argentina. Following the national definition, the general government balance, primary balance, cyclically adjusted primary balance, and expenditure include accrued interest payments.

Bulgaria. Historical ratios of fiscal variables to GDP have been revised compared to the November 2010 *Fiscal Monitor,* reflecting GDP revisions.

Colombia. Historical figures for the overall fiscal balance as reported in the *Monitor* and WEO differ from those published by the Ministry of Finance as they do not include the statistical discrepancy.

Finland. Data on revenue and expenditure of the general government have been revised compared to the November 2010 *Fiscal Monitor* because of different treatment of capital revenue and expenditure.

Greece. Fiscal data revisions for 2006–09 rectify a number of shortfalls in earlier statistics (for details see "Fiscal Policy Assumptions").

Hungary. The cyclically adjusted overall and cyclically adjusted primary balances for 2011 exclude one-off revenues estimated at 10.8 percent of GDP (10.3 percent of potential GDP) as per asset transfer to the general government due to changes to the pension system.

Latvia. In accordance with WEO conventions, the fiscal deficit shown in the *Monitor* includes bank restructuring costs and thus is higher than the deficit in official statistics.

Pakistan. Data are on a fiscal year rather than calendar year basis.

Philippines. Fiscal data are for central government. Historical primary balance data have been revised compared to the November 2010 *Fiscal Monitor,* reflecting IMF staff revisions of interest income data for the national government

Singapore. Data are on a fiscal year rather than calendar year basis.

Switzerland. Swiss fiscal statistics have been revised, compared to the November 2010 *Fiscal Monitor,* with the adoption of the GFSM 2001, full introduction of accrual accounting at the federal level, and other accounting reforms within the cantons and communes. Data submissions at the cantonal and commune level are received with a long and variable lag and are subject to sizable revisions.

Thailand. Data are on a fiscal year rather than calendar year basis.

Turkey. Information on the general government balance, primary balance, and cyclically adjusted primary balance as reported in this *Monitor* and the WEO differ from those published in the authorities' official statistics or country reports, which still include net lending. An additional difference from the authorities' official statistics is the exclusion of privatization receipts in staff projections.

Economy Groupings

The following groupings of economies are used in the *Fiscal Monitor*.

Advanced Economies	Emerging Economies	G-7	G-20	Advanced G-20	Emerging G-20	Euro Area
Australia	Argentina	Canada	Argentina	Australia	Argentina	Austria
Austria	Brazil	France	Australia	Canada	Brazil	Belgium
Belgium	Bulgaria	Germany	Brazil	France	China	Cyprus
Canada	Chile	Italy	Canada	Germany	India	Estonia
Czech Republic	China	Japan	China	Italy	Indonesia	Finland
Denmark	Colombia	United Kingdom	France	Japan	Mexico	France
Estonia	Hungary	United States	Germany	Korea	Russia	Germany
Finland	India		India	United Kingdom	Saudi Arabia	Greece
France	Indonesia		Indonesia	United States	South Africa	Ireland
Germany	Jordan		Italy		Turkey	Italy
Greece	Kazakhstan		Japan			Luxembourg
Hong Kong SAR	Kenya		Korea			Malta
Iceland	Latvia		Mexico			Netherlands
Ireland	Lithuania		Russia			Portugal
Israel	Malaysia		Saudi Arabia			Slovak Republic
Italy	Mexico		South Africa			Slovenia
Japan	Morocco		Turkey			Spain
Korea	Nigeria		United Kingdom			
Netherlands	Pakistan		United States			
New Zealand	Peru					
Norway	Philippines					
Portugal	Poland					
Singapore	Romania					
Slovak Republic	Russia					
Slovenia	Saudi Arabia					
Spain	South Africa					
Sweden	Thailand					
Switzerland	Turkey					
United Kingdom	Ukraine					
United States						

Economy Groupings *(continued)*

Emerging Asia	Emerging Europe	Emerging Latin America	Emerging Middle East and North Africa	Low-Income Economies		Oil Producers
China	Bulgaria	Argentina	Jordan	Afghanistan	Mali	Algeria
India	Estonia	Brazil	Morocco	Armenia	Mauritania	Angola
Indonesia	Hungary	Chile	Tunisia	Bangladesh	Moldova	Azerbaijan
Malaysia	Latvia	Colombia		Benin	Mongolia	Cameroon
Pakistan	Lithuania	Mexico		Bolivia	Mozambique	Chad
Philippines	Poland	Peru		Burkina Faso	Myanmar	Congo, Rep. of
Thailand	Romania			Burundi	Nepal	Ecuador
	Russia			Cambodia	Nicaragua	Equatorial Guinea
	Turkey			Cameroon	Niger	Gabon
	Ukraine			Cape Verde	Rwanda	Indonesia
				Central African Republic	Sao Tome & Principe	Iran
				Chad	Senegal	Kazakhstan
				Comoros	Sierra Leone	Kuwait
				Congo, Dem. Rep. of	St. Lucia	Mexico
				Congo, Rep. of	St Vincent and the Grenadines	Nigeria
				Cote d'Ivoire		Russia
				Djibouti	Sudan	Saudi Arabia
				Dominica	Tajikistan	Sudan
				Eritrea	Tanzania	Syria
				Ethiopia	Togo	Timor-Leste
				Gambia	Uganda	Trinidad and Tobago
				Georgia	Uzbekistan	Venezuela
				Ghana	Vietnam	Vietnam
				Grenada	Yemen	Yemen
				Guinea	Zambia	
				Guinea-Bissau		
				Guyana		
				Haiti		
				Honduras		
				Kyrgyz Republic		
				Lao P.D.R.		
				Lesotho		
				Liberia		
				Madagascar		
				Malawi		
				Maldives		

Economy Groupings *(concluded)*

| ASEAN-5 | Low-Income Economies | | | |
	Africa	Asia	Latin America	Middle East, Eastern Europe, and Central Asia
Indonesia	Benin	Afghanistan	Bolivia	Armenia
Malaysia	Burkina Faso	Bangladesh	Dominica	Djibouti
Philippines	Burundi	Cambodia	Grenada	Georgia
Singapore	Cameroon	Lao P.D.R.	Guyana	Kyrgyz Republic
Thailand	Cape Verde	Maldives	Haiti	Moldova
	Central African Republic	Mongolia	Honduras	Sudan
	Chad	Myanmar	Nicaragua	Tajikistan
	Comoros	Nepal	St. Lucia	Uzbekistan
	Congo, Dem. Rep. of	Vietnam	St. Vincent and the Grenadines	Yemen
	Congo, Rep. of			
	Côte d'Ivoire			
	Eritrea			
	Ethiopia			
	Gambia			
	Ghana			
	Guinea			
	Guinea-Bissau			
	Lesotho			
	Liberia			
	Madagascar			
	Malawi			
	Mali			
	Mauritania			
	Mozambique			
	Niger			
	Rwanda			
	São Tomé and Príncipe			
	Senegal			
	Sierra Leone			
	Tanzania			
	Togo			
	Uganda			
	Zambia			

Statistical Tables

Statistical Table 1. General Government Balance (Percent of GDP)

	2006	2007	2008	2009	2010	2011	2012	2013	2014	2015	2016
Advanced Economies											
Australia	2.0	1.5	-0.5	-4.1	-4.6	-2.5	-0.6	0.0	0.2	0.5	0.7
Austria	-1.6	-0.6	-0.5	-3.5	-4.1	-3.1	-2.9	-2.6	-2.2	-2.2	-2.1
Belgium	0.2	-0.3	-1.3	-6.0	-4.6	-3.9	-4.0	-4.1	-4.1	-4.1	-4.1
Canada	1.6	1.6	0.1	-5.5	-5.5	-4.6	-2.8	-1.6	-0.7	-0.2	0.0
Czech Republic	-2.6	-0.7	-2.7	-5.8	-4.9	-3.7	-3.6	-3.5	-3.4	-3.5	-3.5
Denmark	4.9	4.6	3.2	-2.8	-4.9	-3.6	-2.6	-1.4	-0.5	0.5	1.2
Estonia	3.2	2.9	-2.3	-2.1	0.2	-1.0	-0.7	-0.1	0.9	1.5	1.8
Finland	3.9	5.2	4.2	-2.9	-2.8	-1.2	-1.1	-1.5	-1.4	-1.3	-1.3
France	-2.3	-2.7	-3.3	-7.5	-7.0	-5.8	-4.9	-4.0	-3.0	-2.2	-1.5
Germany	-1.6	0.3	0.1	-3.0	-3.3	-2.3	-1.5	-1.0	-0.4	-0.1	0.0
Greece	-6.1	-6.7	-9.5	-15.4	-9.6	-7.4	-6.2	-4.5	-2.5	-2.1	-2.1
Hong Kong SAR	4.1	7.7	0.1	1.6	4.8	4.6	6.3	6.7	7.0	7.0	7.0
Iceland	6.3	5.4	-0.5	-9.0	-6.8	-4.6	-1.3	1.4	2.1	2.2	1.8
Ireland	2.9	0.1	-7.3	-14.4	-32.2	-10.8	-8.9	-7.4	-4.8	-4.3	-3.8
Israel	-1.2	-0.6	-2.8	-5.6	-4.1	-3.2	-2.2	-1.7	-1.1	-1.0	-1.0
Italy	-3.3	-1.5	-2.7	-5.3	-4.5	-4.3	-3.5	-3.3	-3.2	-3.1	-2.9
Japan	-4.0	-2.4	-4.2	-10.3	-9.5	-10.0	-8.4	-7.8	-7.4	-7.4	-7.4
Korea	2.4	4.2	1.7	0.0	2.4	2.5	2.8	3.0	3.1	3.2	3.1
Netherlands	0.6	0.3	0.6	-5.4	-5.2	-3.8	-2.7	-2.1	-1.8	-1.3	-0.6
New Zealand	2.6	2.5	0.1	-3.3	-6.3	-6.4	-3.7	-2.1	-0.9	-0.1	0.7
Norway	18.5	17.7	19.3	10.4	10.9	13.0	12.7	12.2	11.7	11.4	11.2
Portugal	-4.1	-2.8	-2.9	-9.3	-7.3	-5.6	-5.5	-5.7	-5.8	-5.8	-5.9
Singapore	5.1	10.0	5.3	-0.8	5.3	3.3	3.6	3.7	3.9	3.9	4.1
Slovak Republic	-3.2	-1.8	-2.1	-7.9	-8.2	-5.2	-3.9	-2.9	-2.8	-2.4	-2.2
Slovenia	-0.8	0.3	-0.3	-5.5	-5.2	-4.8	-4.3	-3.5	-3.1	-2.9	-2.9
Spain	2.0	1.9	-4.2	-11.1	-9.2	-6.2	-5.6	-5.0	-4.7	-4.6	-4.6
Sweden	2.4	3.7	2.4	-0.8	-0.2	0.1	0.4	0.9	1.2	1.7	2.0
Switzerland	1.1	1.8	2.0	0.8	0.2	0.3	0.6	0.6	0.9	0.9	0.9
United Kingdom	-2.6	-2.7	-4.9	-10.3	-10.4	-8.6	-6.9	-5.0	-3.4	-2.3	-1.3
United States	-2.0	-2.7	-6.5	-12.7	-10.6	-10.8	-7.5	-5.7	-5.2	-5.5	-6.0
Emerging Economies											
Argentina	-1.0	-2.1	-0.8	-3.8	-1.7	-3.1	-3.1	-3.1	-2.8	-1.8	-1.4
Brazil	-3.5	-2.7	-1.4	-3.1	-2.9	-2.4	-2.6	-2.4	-2.4	-2.3	-2.2
Bulgaria	3.3	3.3	2.9	-0.9	-3.6	-2.6	-1.5	-1.0	-1.2	-0.8	-0.6
Chile	7.9	8.4	4.3	-4.4	-0.4	-0.4	0.4	0.5	0.3	0.4	1.0
China	-0.7	0.9	-0.4	-3.1	-2.6	-1.6	-0.9	-0.5	0.0	0.5	1.0
Colombia	-0.8	-1.0	0.0	-2.6	-2.8	-3.5	-1.1	-1.0	-0.9	-0.6	-0.2
Hungary	-9.3	-5.0	-3.7	-4.3	-4.1	3.9	-4.3	-4.6	-4.2	-3.8	-3.4
India	-5.5	-4.2	-8.0	-10.0	-9.4	-8.3	-7.5	-6.0	-5.6	-5.5	-5.4
Indonesia	0.2	-1.0	0.0	-1.8	-0.6	-1.5	-1.4	-1.4	-1.4	-1.5	-1.5
Jordan	-3.9	-4.5	-4.1	-8.1	-5.4	-6.7	-6.0	-5.3	-4.7	-4.3	-3.9
Kazakhstan	7.2	4.7	1.1	-1.4	1.5	1.8	2.1	2.1	2.3	2.4	2.3
Kenya	-2.5	-3.1	-4.3	-5.4	-6.2	-5.4	-4.6	-4.0	-3.9	-3.2	-2.7
Latvia	-0.5	0.6	-7.5	-7.8	-7.9	-5.3	-1.9	-2.0	-1.3	-1.4	-1.4
Lithuania	-0.4	-1.0	-3.3	-9.2	-7.6	-6.0	-5.5	-5.1	-4.7	-4.4	-4.2
Malaysia	-2.3	-2.6	-3.6	-5.9	-5.1	-5.1	-4.9	-4.7	-4.6	-4.4	-4.3
Mexico	-1.0	-1.3	-1.3	-4.8	-4.1	-1.8	-2.4	-2.3	-2.2	-2.1	-2.0
Morocco	-1.0	1.5	1.2	-2.6	-1.8	-4.8	-4.6	-4.0	-3.7	-3.4	-3.1
Nigeria	10.6	-0.4	4.6	-10.4	-7.2	1.0	3.1	2.4	1.6	0.3	-0.2
Pakistan	-3.7	-4.0	-7.3	-5.2	-6.0	-5.0	-3.5	-3.2	-2.6	-2.2	-1.9
Peru	1.9	3.2	2.2	-2.1	-0.6	-0.5	-0.1	-0.1	-0.1	-0.2	-0.2
Philippines	-1.4	-1.5	-1.3	-3.9	-3.7	-3.3	-2.6	-1.9	-1.9	-1.8	-1.8
Poland	-3.6	-1.9	-3.7	-7.2	-7.9	-5.7	-4.2	-3.7	-3.4	-2.8	-2.6
Romania	-1.4	-3.1	-4.8	-7.3	-6.5	-4.4	-3.0	-2.9	-2.5	-2.3	-2.2
Russia	8.3	6.8	4.9	-6.3	-3.6	-1.6	-1.7	-1.9	-2.8	-3.3	-3.8
Saudi Arabia	24.6	15.8	34.4	-4.7	7.7	12.8	14.1	9.6	10.0	10.0	9.5
South Africa	0.8	1.5	-0.5	-5.2	-5.8	-5.7	-5.0	-4.0	-3.2	-2.1	-0.9
Thailand	2.2	0.2	0.1	-3.2	-2.7	-2.6	-1.7	-1.4	-1.3	-1.1	-1.0
Turkey	0.1	-1.7	-2.4	-5.6	-2.6	-1.7	-1.5	-1.1	-1.1	-1.1	-1.1
Ukraine	-1.4	-2.0	-3.2	-6.2	-5.8	-2.8	-2.5	-2.5	-2.0	-2.0	-2.0
Average	-0.8	-0.6	-2.3	-7.1	-6.0	-5.2	-3.9	-3.1	-2.7	-2.6	-2.5
Advanced	-1.4	-1.1	-3.6	-8.8	-7.7	-7.1	-5.2	-4.1	-3.5	-3.4	-3.5
Emerging	-0.1	0.1	-0.6	-4.9	-3.8	-2.6	-2.2	-1.8	-1.6	-1.4	-1.2
G-7	-2.3	-2.1	-4.6	-10.0	-8.8	-8.6	-6.4	-5.0	-4.4	-4.4	-4.5
G-20	-1.2	-0.9	-2.6	-7.5	-6.3	-5.7	-4.3	-3.4	-3.0	-2.8	-2.8
Advanced G-20	-1.9	-1.7	-4.2	-9.4	-8.2	-8.0	-5.8	-4.5	-4.0	-3.9	-4.0
Emerging G-20	-0.1	0.3	-0.4	-4.8	-3.6	-2.5	-2.1	-1.8	-1.5	-1.3	-1.1

Source: IMF staff estimates and projections. Projections are based on staff assessment of current policies (see section on Fiscal Policy Assumptions).

121

Statistical Table 2. General Government Primary Balance (Percent of GDP)

	2006	2007	2008	2009	2010	2011	2012	2013	2014	2015	2016
Advanced Economies											
Australia	1.7	1.2	-0.8	-4.2	-4.3	-2.1	-0.1	0.4	0.6	0.9	1.0
Austria	0.5	1.5	1.5	-1.4	-1.9	-1.0	-0.5	-0.2	0.3	0.4	0.6
Belgium	3.9	3.3	2.3	-2.6	-1.3	-0.5	-0.4	-0.3	-0.2	-0.1	0.0
Canada	2.2	2.2	0.1	-4.6	-4.9	-4.1	-2.6	-1.6	-0.9	-0.5	0.1
Czech Republic	-1.9	0.1	-1.9	-4.7	-3.9	-2.6	-2.2	-1.9	-1.7	-1.7	-1.7
Denmark	5.5	5.1	3.4	-2.4	-4.6	-3.2	-2.2	-1.0	0.0	1.1	1.9
Estonia	3.4	3.0	-2.2	-1.8	0.4	-0.8	-0.5	0.2	1.1	1.7	2.0
Finland	3.5	4.5	3.2	-3.5	-3.2	-1.8	-1.7	-1.8	-1.5	-1.3	-1.2
France	-0.1	-0.4	-0.8	-5.3	-4.8	-3.3	-2.2	-1.2	0.0	0.9	1.6
Germany	0.8	2.7	2.5	-0.7	-1.1	-0.3	0.5	1.2	1.8	2.2	2.1
Greece	-1.5	-1.9	-4.5	-10.1	-3.2	-0.9	0.9	3.3	5.9	6.2	5.9
Hong Kong SAR	4.2	7.7	0.1	1.6	4.9	4.6	6.3	6.8	7.1	7.1	7.1
Iceland	6.7	5.7	-0.5	-6.5	-2.5	0.3	3.7	6.0	6.0	6.0	6.0
Ireland	3.2	0.3	-6.9	-13.0	-29.7	-7.5	-5.3	-2.2	0.5	1.0	1.5
Israel	2.8	3.4	0.8	-2.2	-0.8	0.5	1.7	2.2	2.6	2.5	2.4
Italy	1.1	3.3	2.2	-1.0	-0.2	0.2	1.2	1.5	1.9	2.1	2.4
Japan	-3.5	-1.9	-3.4	-9.4	-8.4	-8.6	-6.9	-6.2	-5.5	-5.2	-4.9
Korea	3.7	5.6	3.1	1.5	3.6	3.7	3.9	4.0	4.1	4.1	4.0
Netherlands	2.2	2.0	2.1	-3.8	-3.7	-2.2	-1.1	-0.3	0.2	0.7	1.8
New Zealand	4.1	3.9	1.4	-2.0	-4.9	-4.7	-1.8	0.0	1.2	2.0	2.6
Norway	16.3	14.8	16.3	8.0	8.4	10.4	10.1	9.5	9.0	8.6	8.3
Portugal	-1.5	-0.1	-0.1	-6.6	-4.6	-1.6	-0.8	-0.6	-0.3	0.1	0.4
Singapore	4.4	9.3	4.6	-1.5	4.6	2.6	2.9	3.0	3.2	3.3	3.4
Slovak Republic	-2.0	-0.8	-1.2	-6.6	-7.0	-3.6	-2.0	-0.9	-0.7	-0.3	0.0
Slovenia	0.3	1.2	0.5	-4.7	-4.0	-3.4	-2.8	-1.9	-1.4	-1.2	-1.1
Spain	3.3	3.0	-3.1	-9.9	-7.8	-4.6	-3.7	-2.7	-2.1	-1.7	-1.4
Sweden	2.1	3.2	1.7	-1.6	-1.2	-0.9	-0.4	-0.2	0.1	0.5	0.7
Switzerland	2.1	2.7	2.6	1.3	0.7	0.9	1.2	1.2	1.5	1.5	1.4
United Kingdom	-1.1	-1.1	-3.3	-8.5	-7.8	-5.5	-3.9	-2.0	-0.4	0.7	1.5
United States	-0.1	-0.7	-4.5	-10.9	-8.9	-9.0	-5.7	-3.7	-2.7	-2.4	-2.3
Emerging Economies											
Argentina	4.0	2.4	2.7	0.1	1.5	0.3	0.1	-0.2	-0.3	-0.2	0.0
Brazil	3.2	3.4	4.0	2.1	2.4	3.0	3.0	3.0	3.0	3.0	3.0
Bulgaria	4.3	3.9	2.8	-0.5	-3.3	-2.0	-0.8	-0.3	-0.5	-0.1	0.2
Chile	8.1	8.2	4.0	-4.6	-0.3	-0.2	0.2	0.4	0.1	0.3	0.9
China	-0.2	1.3	0.1	-2.6	-2.1	-1.1	-0.5	0.0	0.4	0.9	1.3
Colombia	1.7	1.7	2.2	-0.5	-1.0	-1.5	0.7	0.9	1.0	1.6	1.7
Hungary	-5.6	-1.2	-0.1	-0.2	-0.3	7.5	-0.4	-0.4	0.1	0.6	1.0
India	0.0	1.1	-2.9	-4.9	-4.7	-3.9	-3.0	-3.0	-3.2	-3.2	-3.2
Indonesia	2.6	1.0	1.8	-0.1	0.8	-0.1	0.1	0.0	0.0	-0.1	-0.1
Jordan	-1.2	-1.7	-1.9	-6.0	-3.0	-4.3	-3.7	-3.1	-2.5	-1.6	-0.7
Kazakhstan	6.8	3.8	1.4	-1.5	1.9	1.9	2.2	2.2	2.2	2.3	2.1
Kenya	-0.2	-0.9	-2.1	-3.2	-3.9	-3.1	-2.3	-1.8	-1.7	-1.2	-0.7
Latvia	0.1	1.0	-7.1	-6.7	-6.5	-3.6	-0.1	-0.2	0.5	0.5	0.5
Lithuania	0.1	-0.5	-2.8	-8.1	-6.1	-4.1	-3.5	-3.3	-2.8	-2.5	-2.2
Malaysia	-0.6	-1.1	-1.9	-4.3	-3.6	-3.4	-3.3	-3.3	-3.2	-3.0	-3.0
Mexico	1.7	1.3	1.4	-2.3	-1.8	0.8	0.2	0.4	0.5	0.6	0.7
Morocco	2.2	4.7	3.8	-0.2	0.5	-2.5	-2.2	-1.6	-1.2	-0.9	-0.7
Nigeria	11.7	0.7	5.6	-9.3	-5.7	2.5	4.8	4.5	3.4	1.8	1.2
Pakistan	-0.6	0.2	-2.5	-0.2	-1.6	-0.8	0.3	0.9	1.5	1.3	1.0
Peru	3.7	4.9	3.7	-0.8	0.6	0.7	1.0	1.0	0.9	0.8	0.7
Philippines	4.0	2.6	2.5	-0.2	-0.1	0.4	1.2	1.7	1.6	1.5	1.4
Poland	-1.0	0.4	-1.5	-4.6	-5.3	-2.9	-1.4	-0.7	-0.4	0.2	0.4
Romania	-0.6	-2.4	-4.1	-6.1	-5.1	-2.7	-1.3	-1.2	-0.9	-0.7	-0.5
Russia	8.9	6.8	5.1	-6.0	-3.2	-0.9	-0.9	-1.1	-2.1	-2.6	-3.1
Saudi Arabia	25.6	15.5	33.8	-4.5	7.9	12.7	13.8	8.8	8.5	7.8	6.7
South Africa	3.7	4.3	2.1	-2.7	-3.1	-2.8	-1.9	-0.8	0.2	1.1	2.1
Thailand	3.5	1.2	1.0	-2.4	-1.9	-1.7	-0.8	-0.6	-0.5	-0.3	-0.3
Turkey	5.2	3.2	2.0	-1.0	0.5	0.7	1.1	1.6	1.6	1.6	1.6
Ukraine	-0.7	-1.5	-2.6	-5.1	-4.1	-0.9	-0.6	-0.6	0.1	0.1	0.0
Average	1.2	1.3	-0.5	-5.3	-4.2	-3.3	-2.0	-1.2	-0.7	-0.4	-0.2
Advanced	0.4	0.7	-1.9	-7.1	-5.9	-5.3	-3.3	-2.0	-1.2	-0.8	-0.6
Emerging	2.3	2.3	1.5	-2.8	-1.8	-0.6	-0.1	0.0	0.1	0.2	0.3
G-7	-0.4	-0.1	-2.7	-8.2	-6.9	-6.6	-4.3	-2.9	-1.9	-1.5	-1.3
G-20	0.9	1.1	-0.7	-5.6	-4.4	-3.7	-2.3	-1.5	-0.9	-0.6	-0.4
Advanced G-20	-0.1	0.1	-2.4	-7.6	-6.4	-6.0	-3.8	-2.5	-1.6	-1.2	-1.0
Emerging G-20	2.4	2.5	1.7	-2.7	-1.6	-0.6	-0.1	0.0	0.0	0.2	0.3

Source: IMF staff estimates and projections. Projections are based on staff assessment of current policies (see section on Fiscal Policy Assumptions).

Statistical Table 3. General Government Cyclically Adjusted Overall Balance (Percent of Potential GDP)

	2006	2007	2008	2009	2010	2011	2012	2013	2014	2015	2016
Advanced Economies											
Australia	1.9	1.3	-0.7	-4.0	-4.5	-2.5	-0.8	-0.2	0.0	0.4	0.5
Austria	-2.2	-2.0	-2.2	-2.3	-3.0	-2.4	-2.4	-2.3	-2.2	-2.2	-2.1
Belgium	-1.4	-1.5	-2.2	-3.0	-2.9	-2.8	-3.0	-3.1	-3.2	-3.4	-3.6
Canada	0.8	0.6	0.0	-3.2	-4.0	-3.6	-2.2	-1.4	-0.7	-0.3	0.0
Czech Republic	-2.7	-1.2	-3.1	-4.2	-3.8	-2.8	-3.0	-3.2	-3.3	-3.5	-3.5
Denmark	3.4	3.2	3.0	-0.9	-3.4	-2.7	-1.8	-0.8	0.0	0.9	1.2
Estonia	...	...	...	...	...	...	...	...	...	...	...
Finland	2.7	2.7	2.4	0.8	0.2	0.7	0.1	-0.8	-1.1	-1.2	-1.2
France	-2.7	-3.2	-3.2	-5.5	-5.3	-4.3	-3.7	-3.2	-2.5	-2.0	-1.6
Germany	-2.1	-1.0	-1.0	-1.1	-2.4	-2.1	-1.5	-1.0	-0.6	-0.1	-0.1
Greece	-8.3	-10.2	-13.3	-17.5	-9.5	-6.0	-5.0	-3.8	-2.1	-2.1	-2.1
Hong Kong SAR[1]	0.0	1.3	-0.6	-2.7	-0.9	0.0	0.6	0.9	1.3	1.3	1.3
Iceland	4.5	2.6	-2.0	-5.6	0.7	-2.6	-0.2	1.7	2.3	2.2	1.8
Ireland[2]	-4.2	-7.5	-11.3	-9.6	-8.0	-5.9	-5.7	-4.8	-2.9	-2.9	-2.9
Israel	-1.4	-1.3	-3.7	-5.1	-4.2	-3.5	-2.8	-2.3	-1.8	-1.7	-1.4
Italy	-3.7	-2.3	-2.4	-3.2	-2.8	-2.7	-2.2	-2.3	-2.5	-2.7	-2.9
Japan	-3.9	-2.5	-3.6	-7.0	-7.5	-8.3	-7.4	-7.3	-7.2	-7.3	-7.4
Korea	2.3	4.2	1.8	0.8	2.5	2.5	2.8	3.0	3.1	3.2	3.1
Netherlands	0.1	-1.2	-1.0	-4.4	-4.1	-3.2	-2.2	-1.8	-1.6	-1.2	1.4
New Zealand	1.9	2.0	0.3	-2.1	-3.8	-2.8	-1.8	-0.8	0.0	0.7	
Norway[1]	-2.7	-2.6	-2.8	-4.6	-5.1	-4.8	-4.8	-4.9	-5.0	-5.0	-4.9
Portugal	-3.5	-3.0	-2.7	-7.4	-5.7	-3.2	-2.5	-2.9	-3.2	-3.6	-4.0
Singapore	6.4	11.1	6.2	-2.2	3.4	1.8	2.3	2.4	2.7	4.7	4.9
Slovak Republic	-3.6	-2.5	-2.6	-6.4	-7.0	-4.5	-3.5	-2.7	-2.8	-2.4	-2.2
Slovenia	-1.9	-2.6	-3.9	-4.4	-3.8	-3.6	-3.4	-3.0	-2.9	-2.9	-3.0
Spain	0.7	0.2	-5.3	-9.7	-7.5	-4.7	-4.6	-4.4	-4.5	-4.6	-4.6
Sweden[1]	0.5	1.1	1.2	2.0	1.0	1.6	2.2	2.5	2.6	2.7	2.8
Switzerland[1]	0.8	1.1	1.1	1.1	0.3	0.1	0.5	0.5	0.9	0.9	0.9
United Kingdom	-2.8	-3.3	-5.9	-8.5	-8.3	-6.6	-5.1	-3.5	-2.3	-1.6	-1.1
United States[2]	-2.0	-2.2	-4.6	-6.8	-7.5	-8.1	-5.7	-4.4	-4.3	-4.8	-5.3
Emerging Economies											
Argentina	4.0	1.5	1.9	-1.6	-1.4	-3.7	-3.6	-3.6	-3.2	-2.3	-1.9
Brazil	-3.3	-3.1	-2.1	-2.0	-3.0	-2.5	-2.6	-2.4	-2.4	-2.3	-2.3
Bulgaria	1.8	0.4	-0.3	-0.3	-0.9	0.1	0.8	0.8	0.1	-0.2	-0.4
Chile[1]	0.8	0.6	-1.1	-4.3	-2.0	-1.4	-1.7	-1.4	-0.8	-0.1	0.6
China	-0.6	0.3	-0.9	-3.4	-2.9	-1.8	-1.1	-0.5	0.0	0.5	1.0
Colombia	...	...	...	...	...	...	...	...	...	...	...
Hungary[1]	-11.0	-6.0	-4.3	-0.9	-1.6	-4.8	-2.7	-3.3	-3.3	-3.2	-3.0
India	-5.5	-6.2	-10.2	-11.0	-10.0	-8.8	-7.7	-6.3	-6.2	-6.0	-5.7
Indonesia	0.2	-1.2	-0.2	-1.7	-0.5	-1.5	-1.4	-1.3	-1.4	-1.5	-1.5
Jordan	...	...	...	...	...	...	...	...	...	...	...
Kazakhstan	...	...	...	...	...	...	...	...	...	...	...
Kenya	...	...	...	...	...	...	...	...	...	...	...
Latvia	...	...	...	...	...	...	...	...	...	...	...
Lithuania	...	...	...	...	...	...	...	...	...	...	...
Malaysia	-3.9	-4.2	-5.6	-6.6	-5.3	-5.5	-5.0	-4.7	-4.4	-4.2	-4.0
Mexico	-0.8	-1.6	-1.8	-4.4	-4.1	-2.1	-2.7	-2.6	-2.5	-2.4	-2.5
Morocco	...	...	...	...	...	...	...	...	...	...	...
Nigeria	...	...	...	...	...	...	...	...	...	...	...
Pakistan	...	...	...	...	...	...	...	...	...	...	...
Peru[1]	-0.2	0.3	0.0	-0.4	-0.4	-0.3	-0.2	-0.1	-0.1	0.0	0.0
Philippines	...	...	...	...	...	...	...	...	...	...	...
Poland	-4.1	-3.0	-4.6	-6.8	-7.8	-5.8	-4.4	-3.8	-3.5	-2.8	-2.6
Romania	...	...	...	...	...	...	...	...	...	...	...
Russia	8.0	5.7	3.5	-3.5	-1.8	-0.6	-1.3	-1.7	-2.7	-3.2	-3.7
Saudi Arabia	...	...	...	...	...	...	...	...	...	...	...
South Africa	-0.1	-0.1	-2.1	-4.8	-5.0	-4.9	-4.4	-3.7	-3.1	-2.3	-1.4
Thailand	1.9	0.0	-0.8	-2.2	-2.3	-2.4	-1.7	-1.4	-1.2	-1.1	-1.0
Turkey	-3.0	-4.7	-4.5	-5.0	-3.7	-2.8	-2.8	-2.4	-2.3	-2.4	-2.4
Ukraine	-2.6	-4.1	-3.8	-2.8	-3.1	-1.6	-2.0	-2.5	-2.0	-2.0	-2.0
Average	-1.5	-1.4	-2.9	-5.2	-5.0	-4.6	-3.6	-3.0	-2.7	-2.7	-2.6
Advanced	-1.8	-1.6	-3.3	-5.5	-5.7	-5.5	-4.2	-3.4	-3.1	-3.2	-3.3
Emerging	-1.0	-1.1	-2.4	-4.6	-4.1	-3.2	-2.7	-2.3	-2.1	-1.8	-1.6
G-7	-2.4	-2.2	-3.8	-5.9	-6.4	-6.6	-5.0	-4.1	-3.8	-3.9	-4.1
G-20	-1.5	-1.4	-3.0	-5.2	-5.2	-4.9	-3.8	-3.1	-2.8	-2.8	-2.8
Advanced G-20	-2.0	-1.8	-3.4	-5.6	-6.0	-6.1	-4.5	-3.7	-3.4	-3.5	-3.7
Emerging G-20	-0.8	-1.0	-2.3	-4.6	-4.0	-3.1	-2.7	-2.2	-2.0	-1.8	-1.5

Source: IMF staff estimates and projections. Projections are based on staff assessment of current policies.

[1] For details, see section on Data and Conventions.

[2] Cyclically adjusted overall balance excluding financial sector support recorded above the line.

Statistical Table 4. General Government Cyclically Adjusted Primary Balance (Percent of Potential GDP)

	2006	2007	2008	2009	2010	2011	2012	2013	2014	2015	2016
Advanced Economies											
Australia	1.6	0.9	-1.0	-4.1	-4.2	-2.1	-0.3	0.2	0.5	0.8	0.9
Austria	0.0	0.1	-0.1	-0.2	-0.9	-0.3	-0.1	0.0	0.4	0.4	0.5
Belgium	2.4	2.2	1.4	0.3	0.4	0.6	0.6	0.6	0.6	0.5	0.5
Canada	1.5	1.2	0.0	-2.3	-3.4	-3.2	-2.1	-1.4	-0.9	-0.5	0.1
Czech Republic	-2.0	-0.5	-2.3	-3.2	-2.8	-1.6	-1.7	-1.6	-1.6	-1.7	-1.7
Denmark	4.0	3.7	3.2	-0.5	-3.1	-2.3	-1.4	-0.3	0.5	1.4	1.9
Estonia	...	...	...	...	...	...	...	...	...	...	...
Finland	2.3	2.1	1.4	0.2	-0.2	0.1	-0.5	-1.2	-1.2	-1.2	-1.2
France	-0.4	-0.8	-0.6	-3.5	-3.1	-1.9	-1.1	-0.4	0.4	1.0	1.5
Germany	0.3	1.5	1.4	1.1	-0.3	0.0	0.5	1.2	1.7	2.1	2.0
Greece	-3.4	-5.1	-7.9	-12.0	-3.1	0.3	2.0	3.9	6.2	6.2	5.9
Hong Kong SAR[1]	0.1	1.4	-0.6	-2.7	-0.9	0.1	0.7	1.0	1.3	1.3	1.3
Iceland	4.9	3.0	-2.0	-3.2	4.7	2.1	4.8	6.3	6.2	6.0	6.0
Ireland[2]	-3.9	-7.3	-10.8	-8.3	-5.7	-2.8	-2.3	0.1	2.3	2.4	2.4
Israel	2.6	2.8	-0.1	-1.7	-0.8	0.3	1.2	1.6	1.9	2.0	2.1
Italy	0.7	2.5	2.4	0.9	1.3	1.7	2.4	2.5	2.5	2.4	2.4
Japan	-3.4	-2.0	-2.9	-6.1	-6.4	-7.0	-6.0	-5.6	-5.3	-5.1	-4.9
Korea	3.7	5.6	3.2	2.2	3.7	3.6	3.9	4.0	4.1	4.1	4.0
Netherlands	1.8	0.5	0.6	-2.9	-2.7	-1.6	-0.6	0.0	0.3	0.7	3.9
New Zealand	3.4	3.4	1.6	-0.9	-2.4	-2.2	-0.9	0.2	1.3	2.0	2.6
Norway[1]	-4.9	-5.6	-6.0	-7.0	-7.5	-7.4	-7.5	-7.6	-7.7	-7.8	-7.8
Portugal	-1.0	-0.3	0.1	-4.8	-3.0	0.6	2.0	2.0	2.1	2.2	2.1
Singapore	5.7	10.3	5.5	-2.9	2.7	1.1	1.6	1.7	2.0	4.0	4.2
Slovak Republic	-2.4	-1.4	-1.7	-5.2	-5.9	-2.9	-1.6	-0.8	-0.7	-0.3	0.0
Slovenia	-0.8	-1.6	-3.0	-3.5	-2.7	-2.2	-1.9	-1.4	-1.2	-1.2	-1.2
Spain	2.1	1.3	-4.2	-8.5	-6.1	-3.1	-2.7	-2.2	-1.9	-1.7	-1.4
Sweden[1]	0.2	0.6	0.4	1.2	0.0	0.7	1.4	1.4	1.5	1.5	1.5
Switzerland[1]	1.9	2.0	1.7	1.6	0.8	0.7	1.1	1.0	1.4	1.4	1.4
United Kingdom	-1.3	-1.7	-4.3	-6.8	-5.7	-3.6	-2.1	-0.5	0.7	1.4	1.8
United States[2]	0.0	-0.1	-2.7	-5.1	-5.9	-6.4	-3.9	-2.5	-1.8	-1.7	-1.6
Emerging Economies											
Argentina	9.0	6.1	5.6	2.2	1.9	-0.1	-0.5	-0.6	-0.7	-0.6	-0.5
Brazil	3.4	3.0	3.4	3.1	2.4	2.9	3.0	3.0	3.0	2.9	2.9
Bulgaria	2.8	1.0	-0.3	0.1	-0.6	0.7	1.4	1.5	0.7	0.6	0.3
Chile[1]	1.0	0.4	-1.5	-4.5	-1.9	-1.2	-1.9	-1.5	-0.9	-0.3	0.5
China	-0.2	0.7	-0.3	-2.9	-2.4	-1.3	-0.6	-0.1	0.4	0.9	1.3
Colombia	...	...	...	...	...	...	...	...	...	...	...
Hungary[1]	-7.2	-2.2	-0.6	3.0	2.0	-1.4	1.0	0.8	1.0	1.2	1.4
India	0.0	-0.8	-5.0	-6.0	-5.3	-4.4	-3.2	-3.2	-3.8	-3.7	-3.5
Indonesia	2.6	0.9	1.6	0.0	0.8	0.0	0.1	0.1	0.0	-0.1	-0.1
Jordan	...	...	...	...	...	...	...	...	...	...	...
Kazakhstan	...	...	...	...	...	...	...	...	...	...	...
Kenya	...	...	...	...	...	...	...	...	...	...	...
Latvia	...	...	...	...	...	...	...	...	...	...	...
Lithuania	...	...	...	...	...	...	...	...	...	...	...
Malaysia	-2.2	-2.7	-3.9	-5.0	-3.8	-3.8	-3.4	-3.2	-3.0	-2.8	-2.8
Mexico	2.0	1.1	0.9	-2.0	-1.8	0.4	-0.2	0.0	0.1	0.2	0.2
Morocco	...	...	...	...	...	...	...	...	...	...	...
Nigeria	...	...	...	...	...	...	...	...	...	...	...
Pakistan	...	...	...	...	...	...	...	...	...	...	...
Peru[1]	1.6	2.0	1.6	0.8	0.7	0.8	0.9	1.0	1.0	0.9	0.9
Philippines	...	...	...	...	...	...	...	...	...	...	...
Poland	-1.4	-0.6	-2.4	-4.2	-5.2	-3.1	-1.5	-0.9	-0.5	0.2	0.4
Romania	...	...	...	...	...	...	...	...	...	...	...
Russia	8.5	5.7	3.7	-3.2	-1.5	0.0	-0.5	-0.9	-2.0	-2.5	-3.0
Saudi Arabia	...	...	...	...	...	...	...	...	...	...	...
South Africa	2.9	2.8	0.6	-2.3	-2.5	-2.1	-1.4	-0.5	0.2	0.9	1.6
Thailand	3.2	0.9	0.1	-1.4	-1.6	-1.5	-0.8	-0.6	-0.5	-0.3	-0.3
Turkey	2.4	0.6	0.1	-0.6	-0.6	-0.3	0.0	0.4	0.4	0.3	0.3
Ukraine	-1.9	-3.6	-3.3	-1.7	-1.6	0.3	0.0	-0.6	0.0	0.1	0.0
Average	0.6	0.6	-1.0	-3.3	-3.2	-2.7	-1.7	-1.0	-0.7	-0.5	-0.3
Advanced	-0.1	0.2	-1.6	-3.9	-4.0	-3.7	-2.3	-1.4	-0.8	-0.6	-0.4
Emerging	1.5	1.2	-0.2	-2.5	-2.1	-1.2	-0.7	-0.5	-0.4	-0.2	0.0
G-7	-0.5	-0.2	-1.8	-4.2	-4.6	-4.7	-3.0	-1.9	-1.3	-1.1	-0.9
G-20	0.6	0.6	-0.9	-3.3	-3.3	-1.8	-1.1	-0.8	-0.6	-0.4	-0.4
Advanced G-20	-0.2	0.1	-1.6	-3.9	-4.2	-4.2	-2.6	-1.6	-1.0	-0.8	-0.7
Emerging G-20	1.8	1.4	0.0	-2.4	-2.0	-1.1	-0.6	-0.4	-0.4	-0.2	0.0

Source: IMF staff estimates and projections. Projections are based on staff assessment of current policies.

[1] For details, see section on Data and Conventions.

[2] Cyclically adjusted primary balance excluding financial sector support recorded above the line.

Statistical Table 5. General Government Expenditure (Percent of GDP)

	2006	2007	2008	2009	2010	2011	2012	2013	2014	2015	2016
Advanced Economies											
Australia	34.3	34.0	34.3	37.7	37.2	35.7	35.5	33.5	34.9	33.6	34.5
Austria	49.4	48.5	48.8	52.3	52.3	51.7	51.6	51.3	51.1	51.0	50.9
Belgium	48.5	48.4	50.2	54.2	53.4	53.1	53.1	53.1	53.1	53.1	53.2
Canada	39.3	39.2	39.6	43.8	43.5	42.0	41.4	41.0	40.8	40.8	40.9
Czech Republic	43.7	42.5	42.9	45.9	45.7	44.7	44.4	44.0	44.0	44.0	44.1
Denmark	51.7	50.9	52.0	58.3	58.5	56.9	55.4	54.2	53.5	52.6	51.9
Estonia	34.6	35.4	41.5	47.6	45.5	45.8	44.1	41.5	39.0	38.0	37.0
Finland	49.0	47.2	49.3	56.3	55.1	54.3	54.1	54.4	54.4	54.2	54.2
France	52.7	52.3	52.8	56.2	56.2	55.9	55.3	54.4	53.5	52.7	52.0
Germany	45.3	43.6	43.8	47.5	46.6	45.7	44.8	44.5	43.8	43.6	43.6
Greece	45.2	46.5	49.2	53.2	49.8	49.9	48.4	46.0	41.2	40.1	39.6
Hong Kong SAR	15.4	14.5	18.8	18.0	17.4	19.8	18.1	17.9	17.6	17.3	17.3
Iceland	41.6	42.3	44.6	50.0	49.0	44.0	42.4	40.7	40.2	40.3	40.2
Ireland	33.4	35.8	41.7	48.6	67.7	46.9	45.5	44.7	42.5	42.1	41.5
Israel	45.5	44.8	44.5	44.3	44.2	43.4	42.5	42.1	41.7	41.8	42.0
Italy	48.7	47.9	48.8	51.8	50.5	49.8	48.9	48.6	48.3	48.1	47.9
Japan	34.7	33.4	35.8	40.1	40.3	41.6	40.5	40.5	40.2	40.2	40.2
Korea	20.7	20.8	22.7	24.0	21.3	21.2	21.0	20.9	20.8	20.7	20.8
Netherlands	45.6	44.9	45.8	50.6	50.1	49.5	49.3	49.1	48.8	48.6	48.0
New Zealand	32.5	31.1	32.9	34.4	35.5	35.6	33.7	32.3	31.7	31.0	30.5
Norway	40.3	41.0	40.4	46.1	46.2	44.2	44.4	44.7	45.1	45.3	45.5
Portugal	44.5	43.7	43.6	48.2	48.3	46.6	47.1	47.6	47.7	47.8	47.9
Singapore	15.0	14.2	19.2	19.6	18.0	19.5	19.4	19.2	19.1	18.1	18.3
Slovak Republic	36.6	34.3	35.0	41.5	39.6	38.4	36.6	35.6	35.3	34.8	34.4
Slovenia	42.5	40.3	41.4	46.3	46.2	45.5	44.8	43.9	43.4	43.3	43.3
Spain	38.4	39.2	41.3	45.8	45.0	42.8	42.4	41.7	41.6	41.6	41.7
Sweden	50.6	48.8	49.4	53.0	51.4	50.8	49.5	49.6	49.2	48.7	48.2
Switzerland	35.4	34.2	32.3	34.4	34.4	34.4	34.0	33.9	33.7	33.7	33.7
United Kingdom	40.6	40.3	42.7	47.1	47.0	45.9	44.5	42.8	41.3	40.1	38.7
United States	35.8	36.6	39.0	43.5	41.1	41.2	39.8	39.4	39.8	40.5	41.4
Emerging Economies											
Argentina	30.9	33.7	34.2	39.9	40.6	41.8	41.6	41.4	41.0	40.1	39.9
Brazil	39.5	38.3	37.7	38.8	40.3	38.7	38.8	38.6	38.6	38.6	38.6
Bulgaria	33.6	34.9	35.2	36.2	36.3	35.3	34.3	33.7	33.8	33.4	33.0
Chile	19.7	20.4	22.8	26.4	25.5	24.8	25.1	25.0	25.0	24.8	24.4
China	18.9	18.9	20.0	23.1	22.9	22.4	22.5	22.5	22.6	22.6	22.5
Colombia	28.1	28.2	26.4	29.4	27.5	28.5	26.9	26.8	26.5	25.8	25.2
Hungary	52.0	50.0	48.8	50.4	48.7	47.2	45.5	45.0	44.8	44.6	44.4
India	25.7	26.0	28.2	29.1	27.6	26.9	26.9	25.7	25.3	24.9	24.8
Indonesia	20.1	20.3	21.3	18.3	17.6	18.8	18.6	18.6	18.7	19.0	19.0
Jordan	35.0	35.6	33.3	33.2	29.2	29.9	29.4	28.6	27.9	27.6	27.3
Kazakhstan	20.2	24.6	26.9	23.9	24.1	24.1	24.2	24.2	24.3	24.3	24.4
Kenya	24.7	26.2	27.6	29.0	31.4	31.8	30.9	30.7	30.4	29.4	28.8
Latvia	36.6	35.6	42.9	44.0	44.1	43.4	39.4	37.3	35.7	35.0	34.1
Lithuania	33.9	35.0	37.5	44.1	41.9	41.2	40.8	39.0	38.6	38.2	38.1
Malaysia	27.1	28.0	29.0	33.0	31.1	31.0	30.4	29.9	29.5	29.0	28.5
Mexico	22.5	22.5	24.1	26.9	26.2	24.8	25.6	25.8	25.4	24.9	24.5
Morocco	26.6	26.3	29.9	29.0	27.5	30.1	29.8	29.1	28.7	28.4	28.1
Nigeria	23.2	28.7	28.2	30.4	32.6	28.5	26.0	25.2	25.0	23.3	23.2
Pakistan	18.4	19.3	22.2	19.9	20.5	18.8	18.0	18.4	18.3	18.1	17.8
Peru	18.2	17.7	18.9	21.0	20.7	21.0	20.4	20.5	20.8	20.8	20.8
Philippines	17.5	17.3	17.1	18.6	17.9	17.9	18.3	18.5	18.5	18.5	18.5
Poland	43.9	42.2	43.2	44.4	46.3	45.9	45.2	45.1	44.7	44.1	44.0
Romania	33.7	35.4	37.0	38.7	39.4	37.7	36.7	36.4	35.8	34.8	34.0
Russia	31.1	33.1	34.3	41.4	38.9	38.8	37.6	37.0	37.0	36.9	36.9
Saudi Arabia	32.0	34.6	31.6	45.7	40.8	41.3	37.2	39.3	38.2	37.8	37.6
South Africa	26.9	28.1	30.2	33.0	33.8	34.1	33.7	33.1	32.8	32.3	31.4
Thailand	20.1	21.3	21.2	24.0	23.5	23.6	23.2	23.0	23.0	23.0	22.9
Turkey	32.7	33.3	33.8	37.3	34.8	34.6	34.5	33.9	33.9	34.1	34.2
Ukraine	44.6	43.8	47.4	48.5	49.0	44.9	43.8	43.0	42.3	41.8	41.0
Average	33.1	33.2	34.6	38.1	37.2	36.8	36.1	35.7	35.5	35.5	35.5
Advanced	38.6	38.4	40.2	44.2	43.0	42.8	41.7	41.2	41.1	41.2	41.3
Emerging	25.5	25.9	27.0	29.7	29.1	28.6	28.3	28.1	27.9	27.7	27.6
G-7	39.1	39.1	41.0	45.1	43.8	43.7	42.6	42.1	42.0	42.1	42.4
G-20	32.6	32.7	34.2	37.8	36.7	36.5	35.8	35.4	35.3	35.3	35.4
Advanced G-20	38.2	38.1	40.0	44.0	42.6	42.5	41.4	40.9	40.8	40.9	41.2
Emerging G-20	24.8	25.2	26.2	29.2	28.6	28.1	27.9	27.7	27.5	27.4	27.3

Source: IMF staff estimates and projections. Projections are based on staff assessment of current policies (see section on Fiscal Policy Assumptions).

125

Statistical Table 6. General Government Revenue (Percent of GDP)

	2006	2007	2008	2009	2010	2011	2012	2013	2014	2015	2016
Advanced Economies											
Australia	36.3	35.5	33.8	33.5	32.5	33.2	34.9	33.5	35.1	34.1	35.1
Austria	47.8	47.9	48.2	48.8	48.2	48.6	48.7	48.7	48.8	48.8	48.8
Belgium	48.7	48.1	48.9	48.2	48.8	49.2	49.0	49.0	49.0	49.0	49.1
Canada	40.8	40.7	39.8	38.3	38.0	37.4	38.6	39.4	40.1	40.6	40.9
Czech Republic	41.1	41.8	40.2	40.2	40.8	41.0	40.8	40.6	40.6	40.6	40.6
Denmark	56.6	55.6	55.2	55.4	53.7	53.4	52.8	52.8	53.0	53.1	53.1
Estonia	37.8	38.2	39.2	45.5	45.7	44.8	43.4	41.4	39.9	39.5	38.8
Finland	52.9	52.4	53.5	53.4	52.3	53.1	53.0	52.9	52.9	53.0	53.0
France	50.3	49.6	49.5	48.7	49.2	50.1	50.4	50.4	50.5	50.5	50.5
Germany	43.7	43.8	43.9	44.5	43.3	43.4	43.3	43.5	43.4	43.5	43.5
Greece	39.0	39.8	39.7	37.8	40.2	42.6	42.2	41.5	38.7	38.0	37.6
Hong Kong SAR	19.5	22.2	18.9	19.6	22.2	24.4	24.4	24.7	24.7	24.4	24.4
Iceland	48.0	47.7	44.1	41.1	42.3	39.5	41.1	42.0	42.3	42.4	42.0
Ireland	36.3	35.8	34.3	34.2	35.4	36.1	36.7	37.3	37.7	37.7	37.7
Israel	44.3	44.1	41.7	38.7	40.1	40.2	40.3	40.4	40.6	40.8	40.9
Italy	45.4	46.4	46.1	46.5	46.0	45.5	45.4	45.2	45.2	45.1	45.0
Japan	30.7	31.0	31.6	29.8	30.8	31.7	32.1	32.6	32.8	32.9	32.8
Korea	23.1	25.0	24.4	24.0	23.7	23.7	23.8	23.8	23.9	23.9	23.9
Netherlands	46.2	45.3	46.3	45.2	44.9	45.7	46.6	47.0	47.0	47.4	47.4
New Zealand	35.1	33.6	32.9	31.1	29.2	29.3	30.0	30.3	30.8	31.0	31.2
Norway	58.8	58.7	59.8	56.5	57.1	57.2	57.1	56.9	56.8	56.7	56.6
Portugal	40.5	40.9	40.7	38.9	41.0	40.9	41.6	41.8	41.9	42.0	42.0
Singapore	20.1	24.1	24.5	18.8	23.2	22.7	23.0	22.9	23.0	22.0	22.4
Slovak Republic	33.4	32.5	32.9	33.6	31.4	33.2	32.8	32.7	32.5	32.3	32.2
Slovenia	41.7	40.5	41.1	40.7	41.0	40.7	40.5	40.4	40.4	40.4	40.4
Spain	40.4	41.1	37.1	34.7	35.7	36.5	36.7	36.7	36.9	37.0	37.2
Sweden	53.0	52.5	51.8	52.2	51.2	50.9	49.9	50.4	50.4	50.4	50.2
Switzerland	36.4	36.0	34.3	35.2	34.6	34.7	34.6	34.5	34.6	34.6	34.6
United Kingdom	38.0	37.7	37.8	36.8	36.5	37.3	37.5	37.8	37.8	37.8	37.4
United States	33.8	33.8	32.6	30.8	30.5	30.5	32.3	33.7	34.6	35.0	35.4
Emerging Economies											
Argentina	29.9	31.5	33.4	36.1	38.9	38.7	38.6	38.3	38.2	38.3	38.5
Brazil	35.9	35.7	36.3	35.6	37.4	36.3	36.2	36.2	36.2	36.3	36.3
Bulgaria	37.0	38.2	38.0	35.3	32.7	32.7	32.8	32.7	32.6	32.5	32.5
Chile	27.6	28.8	27.2	22.0	25.1	24.4	25.5	25.5	25.2	25.3	25.4
China	18.2	19.8	19.7	20.0	20.4	20.9	21.6	22.1	22.6	23.1	23.6
Colombia	27.3	27.2	26.5	26.8	24.7	25.1	25.8	25.8	25.6	25.2	25.0
Hungary	42.7	45.1	45.1	46.1	44.6	51.1	41.3	40.4	40.6	40.8	41.0
India	20.2	21.8	20.3	19.2	18.2	18.5	19.4	19.7	19.7	19.4	19.4
Indonesia	20.3	19.3	21.3	16.5	17.1	17.3	17.2	17.3	17.4	17.5	17.4
Jordan	31.1	31.1	29.1	25.1	23.9	23.2	23.4	23.4	23.2	23.3	23.4
Kazakhstan	27.5	29.3	27.9	22.5	25.6	25.9	26.2	26.4	26.5	26.7	26.7
Kenya	22.2	23.1	23.2	23.7	25.2	26.4	26.4	26.7	26.6	26.1	26.0
Latvia	36.1	36.2	35.4	36.2	36.2	38.1	37.5	35.4	34.4	33.6	32.7
Lithuania	33.4	34.0	34.2	34.9	34.3	35.2	35.3	33.9	34.0	33.8	33.9
Malaysia	24.8	25.4	25.4	27.0	26.0	25.9	25.5	25.2	24.9	24.6	24.2
Mexico	21.4	21.2	22.7	22.0	22.1	23.0	23.2	23.5	23.2	22.8	22.5
Morocco	25.6	27.8	31.1	26.4	25.7	25.3	25.2	25.2	25.1	25.0	25.0
Nigeria	33.9	28.4	32.8	19.9	25.5	29.5	29.1	27.6	26.6	23.6	23.0
Pakistan	14.7	15.3	14.9	14.7	14.5	13.9	14.5	15.2	15.8	15.9	15.9
Peru	20.1	20.9	21.1	18.9	20.1	20.6	20.3	20.4	20.7	20.5	20.6
Philippines	16.2	15.8	15.8	14.6	14.2	14.6	15.7	16.6	16.6	16.6	16.6
Poland	40.2	40.3	39.5	37.3	38.4	40.2	41.0	41.5	41.3	41.4	41.5
Romania	32.3	32.3	32.2	31.4	32.8	33.3	33.7	33.6	33.2	32.4	31.8
Russia	39.5	39.9	39.2	35.1	35.3	37.2	35.8	35.0	34.2	33.6	33.1
Saudi Arabia	56.6	50.4	66.0	41.1	48.5	54.1	51.3	48.9	48.2	47.7	47.1
South Africa	27.7	29.6	29.7	27.8	28.0	28.5	28.7	29.1	29.7	30.2	30.6
Thailand	22.3	21.5	21.4	20.8	20.8	21.0	21.5	21.7	21.8	21.9	21.9
Turkey	32.8	31.7	31.5	31.7	32.2	32.9	33.0	32.8	32.9	33.0	33.1
Ukraine	43.2	41.8	44.3	42.2	43.2	42.0	41.2	40.5	40.3	39.8	39.1
Average	32.2	32.6	32.3	31.0	31.2	31.6	32.1	32.5	32.8	32.9	33.0
Advanced	37.2	37.3	36.6	35.4	35.4	35.6	36.5	37.1	37.6	37.7	37.9
Emerging	25.4	26.0	26.3	24.8	25.3	26.0	26.2	26.2	26.3	26.3	26.4
G-7	36.9	36.9	36.3	35.1	35.0	35.1	36.2	37.0	37.5	37.8	37.9
G-20	31.5	31.8	31.6	30.3	30.4	30.8	31.5	32.0	32.3	32.5	32.6
Advanced G-20	36.2	36.4	35.7	34.6	34.4	34.6	35.6	36.3	36.9	37.1	37.2
Emerging G-20	24.7	25.5	25.8	24.4	24.9	25.5	25.8	25.9	26.0	26.1	26.2

Source: IMF staff estimates and projections. Projections are based on staff assessment of current policies (see section on Fiscal Policy Assumptions).

Statistical Table 7. General Government Gross Debt (Percent of GDP)

	2006	2007	2008	2009	2010	2011	2012	2013	2014	2015	2016
Advanced Economies											
Australia	9.8	9.5	11.6	17.6	22.3	24.1	24.8	23.3	23.6	21.8	20.6
Austria	62.1	59.3	62.5	67.5	69.9	70.5	70.7	70.9	70.5	70.1	69.8
Belgium	88.0	84.2	89.8	96.3	97.1	97.3	97.4	97.8	98.2	98.3	98.8
Canada	70.3	66.5	71.3	83.4	84.0	84.2	83.1	81.0	78.5	75.6	72.6
Czech Republic	29.4	29.0	30.0	35.4	39.6	41.7	43.4	44.5	45.6	46.5	47.6
Denmark	41.0	34.1	42.2	41.5	44.3	45.6	46.5	46.3	45.1	43.0	40.2
Estonia	4.4	3.7	4.6	7.2	6.6	6.3	6.0	5.7	5.4	5.2	4.9
Finland	39.7	35.2	34.1	43.8	48.4	50.8	52.7	55.0	57.3	59.2	61.1
France	63.6	63.9	67.7	78.3	81.8	85.0	86.9	87.6	87.1	85.9	84.1
Germany	67.6	64.9	66.3	73.5	80.0	80.1	79.4	77.9	75.8	73.8	71.9
Greece	106.1	105.1	110.3	126.8	142.0	152.3	157.7	157.0	152.5	149.4	145.5
Hong Kong SAR	1.8	1.5	1.3	3.4	4.6	4.3	4.0	3.8	3.6	3.4	3.2
Iceland	30.1	28.6	69.7	91.7	96.6	103.2	97.1	92.1	85.3	80.9	73.8
Ireland	24.8	25.0	44.4	65.5	96.1	114.1	121.5	125.8	125.0	123.5	121.5
Israel	84.6	77.7	76.8	80.4	77.9	73.0	70.0	67.5	64.8	62.6	60.6
Italy	106.6	103.6	106.3	116.1	119.0	120.3	120.0	120.1	119.3	118.7	118.0
Japan	191.3	187.7	195.0	216.3	220.3	229.1	233.4	238.0	242.4	246.7	250.5
Korea	30.1	29.7	29.0	32.6	30.9	28.8	26.9	25.1	23.3	21.5	19.8
Netherlands	47.4	45.3	58.2	60.8	63.7	65.6	66.5	66.7	66.5	65.7	64.4
New Zealand	19.9	17.4	20.3	26.1	31.6	35.8	36.4	36.5	36.1	33.7	31.7
Norway	60.5	58.6	56.7	54.3	54.3	54.3	54.3	54.3	54.3	54.3	54.3
Portugal	63.9	62.7	65.3	76.1	83.3	90.6	94.6	97.5	100.8	103.7	106.5
Singapore	86.8	85.9	97.2	105.0	97.2	93.7	91.3	88.5	86.1	83.9	82.9
Slovak Republic	30.5	29.6	27.8	35.4	42.0	45.1	46.2	46.5	46.8	46.2	45.7
Slovenia	26.7	23.4	22.5	35.4	37.2	42.3	44.9	46.7	48.0	49.3	50.6
Spain	39.6	36.1	39.8	53.2	60.1	63.9	67.1	69.9	72.1	74.1	75.9
Sweden	45.2	40.1	37.7	41.9	39.6	37.3	34.9	32.2	29.3	26.2	22.8
Switzerland	64.4	57.2	54.8	54.9	55.0	52.7	51.2	49.7	48.3	47.0	45.7
United Kingdom	43.1	43.9	52.0	68.3	77.2	83.0	86.5	87.4	86.5	84.4	81.3
United States	61.1	62.2	71.2	84.6	91.6	99.5	102.9	105.6	107.5	109.4	111.9
Emerging Economies											
Argentina	76.4	67.7	58.1	57.6	47.8	40.7	36.7	35.8	35.3	34.3	31.4
Brazil	66.7	65.2	70.7	67.9	66.1	65.7	65.0	63.8	62.1	60.3	58.6
Bulgaria	23.4	18.6	15.5	15.6	18.0	19.7	20.0	19.7	18.8	17.3	15.2
Chile	5.3	4.1	5.2	6.2	8.8	10.9	10.2	9.6	9.0	8.5	8.0
China	16.2	19.6	17.0	17.7	17.7	17.1	16.3	15.0	13.4	10.8	9.7
Colombia	36.8	32.7	31.0	36.2	36.5	36.3	35.4	34.0	32.7	31.5	29.9
Hungary	65.8	66.1	72.3	78.4	80.4	76.6	76.9	77.1	76.8	76.0	75.3
India	78.9	75.8	74.4	75.8	72.2	70.8	69.9	67.5	65.4	63.5	61.8
Indonesia	40.4	36.9	33.2	28.6	26.9	25.4	24.0	22.8	21.8	21.1	19.9
Jordan	73.5	71.0	58.1	61.4	60.5	61.9	62.1	61.9	61.7	61.3	60.5
Kazakhstan	6.7	5.9	6.7	10.4	11.4	12.6	14.1	15.3	16.2	17.4	18.1
Kenya	46.8	46.1	46.2	49.4	50.5	52.3	50.9	49.6	48.9	48.3	47.0
Latvia	9.9	7.8	17.1	32.8	39.9	42.5	41.0	39.8	38.1	36.8	36.2
Lithuania	18.0	16.9	15.6	29.6	38.7	43.5	45.4	47.7	49.5	50.9	52.1
Malaysia	43.2	42.7	42.8	55.4	54.2	55.1	55.8	56.5	56.9	57.2	57.3
Mexico	38.4	37.8	43.0	44.6	42.7	42.3	42.1	42.0	41.9	41.6	41.4
Morocco	59.4	54.6	48.2	47.7	49.9	52.8	53.8	54.0	53.8	53.0	51.7
Nigeria	11.8	12.8	11.6	15.2	16.4	16.2	18.5	21.1	18.6	16.7	14.8
Pakistan	56.4	54.6	58.7	57.3	56.8	54.1	50.9	49.5	47.8	44.5	41.2
Peru	33.2	30.9	25.0	26.6	24.3	22.5	20.7	19.3	18.1	17.0	16.1
Philippines	55.4	47.8	48.7	49.2	47.3	47.0	46.0	44.3	42.8	41.4	40.1
Poland	47.7	45.0	47.1	50.9	55.7	56.6	57.3	57.5	57.4	56.5	55.5
Romania	18.4	19.8	21.3	29.6	35.2	37.8	37.7	37.5	36.8	36.0	35.0
Russia	9.0	8.5	7.9	11.0	9.9	8.5	8.8	9.5	11.3	13.5	15.9
Saudi Arabia	27.3	18.5	13.2	16.0	10.8	8.3	7.1	6.2	5.3	4.4	3.7
South Africa	32.6	28.3	27.3	31.5	36.3	40.5	42.8	43.8	43.5	42.0	38.7
Thailand	42.0	38.3	37.3	45.2	44.1	43.7	44.0	43.9	43.8	43.5	43.0
Turkey	46.1	39.4	39.5	45.5	41.7	39.4	37.6	36.4	35.4	34.7	34.0
Ukraine	14.8	12.3	20.5	35.3	40.5	42.6	43.5	41.5	39.5	35.0	30.7
Average	58.4	57.6	60.8	68.5	71.2	73.7	74.7	75.2	75.2	75.0	74.9
Advanced	74.1	73.1	79.2	91.3	96.6	101.6	103.7	105.2	106.0	106.6	107.3
Emerging	36.7	36.1	35.3	37.0	36.0	35.3	34.6	33.7	32.6	31.2	30.2
G-7	82.9	82.3	89.3	103.0	108.8	114.9	117.4	119.3	120.5	121.4	122.5
G-20	61.1	60.6	64.0	71.9	74.5	77.3	78.3	78.8	78.9	78.8	78.9
Advanced G-20	78.5	78.0	84.5	97.5	102.9	108.5	110.8	112.5	113.5	114.2	115.1
Emerging G-20	36.6	36.3	35.2	36.1	34.6	33.6	32.8	31.7	30.5	29.1	28.1

Source: IMF staff estimates and projections. Projections are based on staff assessment of current policies (see section on Fiscal Policy Assumptions).

Statistical Table 8. General Government Net Debt (Percent of GDP)

	2006	2007	2008	2009	2010	2011	2012	2013	2014	2015	2016
Advanced Economies											
Australia	-6.4	-7.3	-5.4	0.0	5.5	7.8	8.3	7.6	7.4	6.4	5.3
Austria	42.7	39.8	40.7	47.3	49.8	50.7	51.1	51.5	51.3	51.1	50.9
Belgium	77.2	73.3	73.9	80.1	81.5	82.3	83.0	83.9	84.9	85.5	86.5
Canada	26.3	22.9	22.4	28.4	32.2	35.1	36.3	36.3	35.5	34.4	33.0
Czech Republic	...	...	...	...	...	...	...	...	...	...	...
Denmark	1.9	-3.8	-6.5	-4.2	0.9	4.4	6.9	8.1	8.3	7.5	6.0
Estonia	-4.9	-5.6	-3.3	-1.3	-1.0	0.1	0.8	0.9	-0.1	-1.6	-3.3
Finland	-69.5	-72.6	-52.4	-62.7	-56.8	-52.6	-49.1	-45.6	-42.3	-39.4	-36.6
France	59.3	59.3	61.8	71.3	76.0	79.2	81.1	81.8	81.3	80.1	78.3
Germany	52.7	50.1	49.7	55.9	53.8	54.7	54.7	53.9	52.6	52.6	52.6
Greece	...	...	...	...	...	...	...	...	...	...	...
Hong Kong SAR	...	...	...	...	...	...	...	...	...	...	...
Iceland	7.8	10.8	41.7	59.8	67.6	69.9	66.8	62.2	57.0	51.8	47.2
Ireland	12.2	12.2	23.0	38.0	69.4	95.2	104.3	110.3	108.7	106.4	103.5
Israel	74.0	69.0	70.0	73.9	73.2	69.5	67.4	65.3	62.8	60.7	58.8
Italy	89.8	87.3	89.2	97.1	99.6	100.6	100.4	100.2	100.0	99.5	98.9
Japan	84.3	81.5	96.5	110.0	117.5	127.8	135.1	142.4	149.6	156.8	163.9
Korea	28.3	27.7	27.8	31.1	29.6	27.5	25.7	24.0	22.3	20.6	18.9
Netherlands	24.5	21.6	20.6	23.0	27.5	30.5	32.3	33.5	34.3	34.6	34.1
New Zealand	0.2	-5.7	-4.8	-0.8	4.6	10.4	13.6	14.7	14.8	13.5	11.7
Norway	-136.3	-142.5	-126.1	-148.8	-156.4	-157.3	-163.7	-170.5	-176.4	-181.5	-186.0
Portugal	58.8	58.1	61.1	71.9	79.1	86.3	90.4	93.3	96.6	99.5	102.3
Singapore	...	...	...	...	...	...	...	...	...	...	...
Slovak Republic	...	...	...	...	...	...	...	...	...	...	...
Slovenia	...	...	...	...	...	...	...	...	...	...	...
Spain	30.5	26.5	30.4	41.8	48.8	52.6	55.7	58.5	60.7	62.7	64.6
Sweden	-13.9	-17.1	-11.9	-15.8	-14.6	-13.8	-13.5	-13.7	-14.2	-15.1	-16.3
Switzerland	64.2	56.9	53.0	53.1	53.2	51.0	49.6	48.1	46.8	45.5	44.3
United Kingdom	38.0	38.2	45.6	60.9	69.4	75.1	78.6	79.5	78.7	76.5	73.5
United States	41.9	42.6	48.4	59.9	64.8	72.4	76.7	79.3	81.3	83.4	85.7
Emerging Economies											
Argentina	...	...	...	...	...	...	...	...	...	...	...
Brazil	47.0	45.1	38.1	42.2	40.2	40.0	39.4	38.9	38.2	37.5	36.8
Bulgaria	-10.4	-10.2	-10.6	-10.0	-4.2	-1.7	-1.0	-0.8	-1.4	-2.6	-4.3
Chile	-1.7	-9.9	-17.5	-11.6	-11.5	-11.4	-12.3	-13.0	-13.4	-13.9	-15.3
China	...	...	...	...	...	...	...	...	...	...	...
Colombia	26.3	22.7	21.1	27.2	28.5	29.6	28.8	27.8	26.8	26.0	24.7
Hungary	62.7	62.6	63.4	69.8	73.4	70.9	71.4	72.0	72.0	71.5	71.0
India	...	...	...	...	...	...	...	...	...	...	...
Indonesia	...	...	...	...	...	...	...	...	...	...	...
Jordan	66.3	65.1	52.9	55.8	55.1	57.0	57.6	57.8	57.9	57.7	57.2
Kazakhstan	-10.7	-14.4	-13.7	-11.1	-10.7	-10.5	-11.5	-12.6	-13.6	-14.5	-14.8
Kenya	42.1	41.5	41.2	44.3	45.5	47.2	45.9	44.5	43.9	43.3	42.0
Latvia	7.4	4.7	11.3	21.5	30.7	34.4	34.5	34.6	34.0	33.5	33.0
Lithuania	11.0	11.2	12.8	23.5	31.4	36.7	39.1	41.7	43.9	45.7	47.1
Malaysia	...	...	...	...	...	...	...	...	...	...	...
Mexico	32.4	31.1	35.5	38.9	38.1	36.8	36.8	36.8	36.9	36.7	36.7
Morocco	56.8	53.1	47.5	47.0	49.2	52.1	53.1	53.3	53.1	52.3	51.7
Nigeria	-13.7	0.8	-3.2	15.1	18.3	10.9	5.5	1.8	-1.7	-1.7	-1.2
Pakistan	...	...	...	...	...	...	...	...	...	...	...
Peru	...	...	...	...	...	...	...	...	...	...	...
Philippines	...	...	...	...	...	...	...	...	...	...	...
Poland	15.0	10.2	9.9	14.8	21.4	25.2	27.1	28.5	28.3	27.5	26.5
Romania	...	...	...	...	...	...	...	...	...	...	...
Russia	...	...	...	...	...	...	...	...	...	...	...
Saudi Arabia	1.7	-17.1	-45.8	-50.3	-49.8	-51.0	-62.8	-70.2	-75.9	-80.7	-84.5
South Africa	29.7	24.8	23.4	27.3	32.3	36.6	39.5	40.8	40.8	40.0	37.3
Thailand	...	...	...	...	...	...	...	...	...	...	...
Turkey	38.5	32.2	32.8	37.9	35.0	32.7	30.6	29.1	27.8	26.7	25.6
Ukraine	11.7	10.1	18.3	31.9	38.4	41.0	42.5	40.8	38.8	34.3	30.1
Average	43.1	41.5	45.2	53.9	57.7	62.1	64.4	65.9	66.8	67.6	68.5
Advanced	46.4	45.4	50.6	60.3	64.8	70.2	73.3	75.3	76.7	78.0	79.2
Emerging	28.5	25.0	21.7	26.2	26.9	26.8	25.7	24.8	23.8	22.7	21.6
G-7	52.4	51.8	57.7	68.6	73.3	79.5	83.2	85.6	87.4	89.1	90.8
G-20	47.5	46.3	50.3	59.6	63.2	68.0	70.6	72.2	73.4	74.5	75.6
Advanced G-20	49.7	49.1	54.6	65.0	69.4	75.2	78.5	80.7	82.2	83.7	85.3
Emerging G-20	35.2	30.6	26.0	29.2	28.2	27.7	26.1	25.0	24.0	22.9	21.8

Source: IMF staff estimates and projections. Projections are based on staff assessment of current policies (see section on Fiscal Policy Assumptions).

Statistical Table 9. Structural Fiscal Indicators
(Percent of GDP, unless indicated otherwise)

	Pension Spending, Change 2010–30	NPV of Pension Spending Change 2010–50	Health Care Spending, Change 2010–30	NPV of Health Care Spending Change 2010–50	Gross Funding Need, 2011	Average Maturity, 2010 (Years)	Debt-to-Average Maturity, 2010	Proj. Interest Rate–Growth Differential, 2011–15 (Percent)	Precrisis Overall Balance, 2000–07	Postcrisis Overall Balance, 2011–16	Nonresident Holding of Marketable Central Gov. Debt 2010 (Percent of Total)	Nonresident Holding of General Gov. Debt, 2010 (Percent of Total)
Advanced Economies												
Australia	1.2	34.0	2.1	67.0	4.5	5.5	4.1	0.3	1.6	-0.3	71.9	43.4
Austria	1.1	25.7	3.2	104.6	7.8	7.8	8.9	0.3	-1.6	-2.5	78.1	87.5
Belgium	3.6	92.5	2.0	64.3	22.4	6.6	14.7	0.1	-0.4	-4.0	58.0	68.3
Canada	1.6	35.8	2.0	61.1	18.5	6.3	13.4	-0.2	1.1	-1.7	14.3	19.6
Czech Republic	0.0	18.9	0.6	17.5	11.0	6.6	6.0	-0.6	-4.1	-3.5	…	33.4
Denmark	1.2	29.4	0.8	21.5	9.3	8.1	5.5	-0.5	2.3	-1.1	43.4	41.8
Estonia	-0.8	-22.8	1.1	37.3	1.0	11.5	0.6	-0.9	1.5	0.4	…	86.8
Finland	3.2	76.7	2.5	76.4	11.2	5.2	9.3	-1.1	4.0	-1.3	93.2	89.3
France	0.7	16.5	1.5	43.8	20.4	7.3	11.2	0.0	-2.7	-3.5	67.3	66.3
Germany	1.3	34.7	0.9	28.1	11.4	6.7	11.9	0.2	-2.2	-0.9	52.9	52.8
Greece	0.3	24.1	3.2	106.9	24.0	7.8	18.2	3.2	-5.5	-4.1	69.6	61.5
Hong Kong SAR	…	…	…	…	-3.2	3.1	1.5	-6.2	-0.1	6.5	…	13.8
Iceland	2.1	56.6	3.2	105.0	18.8	5.3	18.3	1.3	1.5	0.3	61.6	59.4
Ireland	1.3	46.1	0.7	23.2	19.4	7.0	13.7	1.1	1.5	-6.7	85.2	…
Israel	…	…	…	…	22.0	4.7	16.5	-0.1	-3.2	-1.7	…	17.0
Italy	0.8	22.0	0.6	18.8	22.8	6.8	17.6	1.0	-2.9	-3.4	44.3	47.0
Japan	-0.2	6.6	1.0	27.5	55.8	6.2	35.6	0.0	-5.9	-8.1	4.4	6.9
Korea	1.7	54.5	3.2	111.9	8.9	4.1	7.5	-3.0	2.6	3.0	…	11.5
Netherlands	2.8	77.8	2.6	79.3	19.9	6.2	10.2	0.7	-0.6	-2.1	70.0	66.4
New Zealand	2.0	54.9	3.0	95.9	15.0	4.5	7.0	0.6	3.0	-2.1	44.0	44.0
Norway	3.1	86.5	1.7	52.0	-1.2	2.8	19.6	-3.1	13.5	12.0	44.4	44.4
Portugal	0.7	18.9	3.5	116.5	21.6	6.6	12.7	3.8	-3.6	-5.8	74.9	66.1
Singapore[1]	…	…	…	…	…	2.9	34.1	-5.3	4.9	3.8	…	…
Slovak Republic	0.7	25.8	1.2	37.1	14.5	5.6	7.6	-1.1	-5.0	-3.2	33.7	31.5
Slovenia	3.2	110.4	0.7	22.2	7.2	6.9	5.4	-0.4	-1.0	-3.6	…	63.5
Spain	0.5	26.4	1.6	51.5	19.3	6.7	9.0	1.0	0.3	-5.1	45.5	49.6
Sweden	-0.1	-6.8	0.4	11.7	5.4	6.6	6.0	-1.9	1.4	1.0	40.1	45.2
Switzerland	…	…	3.9	127.7	2.9	6.6	8.3	-0.6	0.1	0.7	…	7.5
United Kingdom	0.9	23.4	3.3	113.3	15.7	13.8	5.6	-0.8	-1.9	-4.6	34.0	26.7
United States	1.1	23.9	5.1	164.5	28.8	5.3	17.2	-0.8	-3.1	-6.8	51.0	31.9

Statistical Table 9. Structural Fiscal Indicators (continued)

	Pension Spending, Change 2010–30	NPV of Pension Spending Change 2010–50	Health Care Spending, Change 2010–30	NPV of Health Care Spending 2010–50	Gross Funding Need, 2011	Average Maturity, 2010 (Years)	Debt-to-Average Maturity, 2010	Proj. Interest Rate–Growth Differential, 2011–15 (Percent)	Precrisis Overall Balance, 2000–07	Postcrisis Overall Balance, 2011–16	Nonresident Holding of Marketable Central Gov. Debt 2010 (Percent of Total)	Nonresident Holding of General Gov. Debt, 2010 (Percent of Total)
Emerging Economies												
Argentina	0.4	20.3	1.5	51.8	5.2	13.7	3.5	-13.1	-4.7	-2.6	...	13.7
Brazil	1.3	67.4	1.6	52.0	19.3	5.0	13.3	-0.3	-3.5	-2.4	...	4.8
Bulgaria	-0.5	-2.5	1.3	44.6	3.8	4.6	3.9	-1.2	1.1	-1.3	...	43.6
Chile	...	...	1.5	50.5	1.9	7.4	1.2	-3.1	7.0	0.4	...	22.6
China	0.2	7.6	0.8	27.8	4.4	8.6	2.1	-8.3	-1.8	-0.2	...	...
Colombia	...	...	...	...	7.2	6.6	5.6	2.0	-1.8	-1.2	...	29.3
Hungary	-0.3	6.3	1.6	51.9	14.9	3.0	26.5	-0.1	-6.6	-2.7	...	60.7
India	0.4	5.8	0.4	12.6	12.6	9.4	7.7	-7.4	-7.7	-6.4	...	6.5
Indonesia	0.4	14.4	0.5	15.6	2.8	9.1	3.0	-4.9	-1.0	-1.4	...	54.2
Jordan	...	...	...	...	6.9	3.7	16.3	-4.2	-3.5	-5.1	...	29.1
Kazakhstan	...	...	...	...	4.0	6.6	1.7	-7.1	4.1	2.2	...	22.1
Kenya	...	...	...	...	...	5.0	10.0	-6.0	-1.9	-4.0	...	0.0
Latvia	0.8	16.3	1.0	34.7	11.3	3.3	12.1	-0.8	-1.4	-2.2	...	81.2
Lithuania	1.7	50.7	1.5	49.4	12.4	4.5	8.6	-1.5	-1.8	-5.0	...	74.6
Malaysia	1.7	47.5	0.8	25.8	9.1	4.6	11.8	-3.5	-3.8	-4.7	...	4.0
Mexico	2.1	49.3	1.1	37.7	9.9	5.7	7.5	-0.4	-2.1	-2.1	...	18.9
Morocco	...	...	...	...	11.8	5.7	8.8	-2.7	-2.2	-3.9	...	19.9
Nigeria	...	...	...	...	...	4.4	3.7	-3.5	3.4	1.4	...	...
Pakistan	0.4	13.8	0.2	8.3	24.1	2.3	24.4	-5.8	-3.0	-3.1	...	...
Peru	...	...	...	...	0.8	15.9	1.5	-2.7	-0.7	-0.2	...	53.1
Philippines	0.5	14.6	0.5	15.6	15.6	8.7	5.5	-0.7	-3.6	-2.2	...	...
Poland	-1.4	-42.4	1.8	58.7	14.0	5.1	11.0	-0.9	-4.3	-3.7	...	43.5
Romania	2.0	74.2	1.3	43.0	13.3	1.9	18.4	-3.2	-2.6	-2.9	...	42.5
Russia	4.6	126.4	1.1	36.7	4.2	6.5	1.5	-1.3	4.6	-2.5	...	24.1
Saudi Arabia	1.4	53.0	1.0	35.5	...	3.5	3.1	-3.8	10.8	11.0	...	...
South Africa	0.6	16.7	1.1	36.5	8.7	8.8	4.1	-0.9	-0.6	-3.5	...	26.2
Thailand	...	...	1.1	36.5	9.7	6.0	7.2	-4.1	-0.4	-1.5	...	5.4
Turkey	3.2	70.3	1.3	44.0	12.6	4.1	10.1	-0.4	-4.9	-1.3	...	26.3
Ukraine	6.0	172.6	1.2	38.8	8.8	5.0	8.1	-6.1	-2.4	-2.3	...	39.2
Average												
Advanced	1.0	25.8	3.0	96.0	24.8	6.3	16.1	-0.4	-2.2	-4.5	45.2	35.1
Emerging	0.9	28.6	0.9	29.5	8.2	7.4	5.7	-5.0	-2.0	-1.8	...	20.4
G-7	0.9	22.3	3.3	104.5	28.6	6.5	17.9	-0.4	-3.1	-5.5	42.2	32.8
G-20	1.0	28.7	2.4	78.7	19.8	6.8	12.5	-2.3	-2.1	-3.5	...	30.2
Advanced G-20	0.9	24.0	3.2	103.8	27.0	6.4	17.0	-0.5	-2.7	-5.0	43.1	32.2
Emerging G-20	1.1	37.2	1.2	33.2	6.6	7.5	4.4	-5.7	-1.0	-0.7	...	21.8

Sources: April 2011 WEO; Bloomberg; country authorities; OECD; Joint BIS-IMF-OECD-WB Statistics on External Debt; and IMF staff calculations.

Note: NPV = Net present value. For the NPV calculations, a discount rate of 1 percent a year is used in excess of GDP growth for each country. *Pension projections* are based on IMF (2010b) staff estimates. Projections do not take into account recent reforms (or plans for reforms) in the following countries: Estonia, France, Hungary, Ireland, Latvia, Poland, Romania, and Russia. Pension spending projections for Spain and Greece reflect recent reforms. For Spain, the estimates assume that future revisions to the sustainability factor would offset expected increases in life expectancy after 2030. For Greece, the estimates for the main pension funds are from the Greek Actuarial Authority and also assume that supplementary pensions grow in line with other pensions. *Health care spending projections* are based on IMF (2010a) staff estimates. Projections do not take into account recent reforms (or plans for reforms) in the following countries: France, Germany, Greece, Ireland, Italy, Portugal, Spain, and the United Kingdom. *Gross funding needs* are defined as the projected overall balance and maturing government debt in 2011. For advanced economies data are from Bloomberg and for emerging economies from IMF staff. *Average maturity* data are from Bloomberg. Data for *projected interest rate–growth differential* and the *overall balance* are based on the April 2011 WEO. *Nonresident holding of central government debt* (*marketable securities*) data are from national authorities and from the OECD (2010d) (general government for Germany, Italy, and Spain). *Nonresident holding of general government debt data* are from the Joint External Debt Statistics, 2010:Q3. They represent all government debt (marketable as well as nonmarketable) at the general government level (see also April 2011 GFSR).

[1] Singapore's general government debt is covered by financial assets and issued to develop the bond market.

Glossary

Automatic stabilizers. Change in the cyclical balance.

Credit default swap (CDS) spreads. The spread on a credit default swap refers to the annual amount (in basis points of the notional amount) that the protection buyer must pay the seller over the length of the contract to protect the underlying asset against a credit event.

Cyclical balance. Cyclical component of the overall fiscal balance, computed as the difference between cyclical revenues and cyclical expenditure. The latter is typically computed using country-specific elasticities of aggregate revenue and expenditure series with respect to the output gap. Where these are unavailable, standard elasticities (0,1) are assumed for expenditure and revenue, respectively.

Cyclically adjusted balance (CAB). Overall balance minus cyclical balance.

Cyclically adjusted (CA) expenditure and revenue. Revenue and expenditure adjusted for the effect of the economic cycle (i.e., net of cyclical revenue and expenditure).

Cyclically adjusted primary balance (CAPB). Cyclically adjusted balance excluding net interest payments

Expenditure elasticity. Elasticity of expenditure with respect to the output gap.

Fiscal stimulus. Discretionary fiscal policy actions adopted in response to the financial crisis.

General government. The general government sector consists of all government units and all nonmarket, nonprofit institutions that are controlled and mainly financed by government units comprising the central, state, and local governments. The general government sector does not include public corporations or quasi-corporations.

Gross debt. All liabilities that require future payment of interest and/or principal by the debtor to the creditor. This includes debt liabilities in the form of Special Drawing Rights (SDRs), currency and deposits, debt securities, loans, insurance, pensions and standardized guarantee schemes, and other accounts payable. The term "public debt" is used in this *Monitor*, for simplicity, as synonymous with gross debt of the general government, unless otherwise specified. (Strictly speaking, the term "public debt" refers to the debt of the public sector as a whole, which includes financial and nonfinancial public enterprises and the central bank.)

Gross financing needs. Overall new borrowing requirement plus debt maturing during the year.

Net debt. Gross debt minus financial assets, including those held by the broader public sector: for example, social security funds held by the relevant component of the public sector, in some cases.

Output gap. Deviation of actual from potential GDP, in percent of potential GDP.

Overall fiscal balance (also "headline" fiscal balance). Net lending/borrowing, defined as the difference between revenue and total expenditure, using the 2001 edition of the IMF's *Government Finance Statistics Manual* (GFSM 2001). Does not include policy lending. For some countries, the overall balance continues to be based on GFSM 1986, in which it is defined as total revenue and grants minus total expenditure and net lending.

Policy lending. Transactions in financial assets that are deemed to be for public policy purposes but are not part of the overall balance.

Primary balance. Overall balance excluding net interest payment (interest expenditure minus interest revenue).

Public debt. See gross debt.

Public sector. The public sector consists of the general government sector plus government-controlled entities, known as public corporations, whose primary activities are commercial.

Relative asset swap (RAS) spreads. Relative asset swap spreads measure the difference between benchmark government bond yields and the interest rate on the fixed-rate arm of an interest rate swap in the same currency and of the same maturity (usually 10 years) as the bond.

Revenue elasticity. Elasticity of revenue with respect to the output gap.

Structural fiscal balance. Cyclically adjusted balance, corrected for one-off and other factors, such as asset and commodity prices and output compositions effects.

Tax expenditures. Government revenues that are foregone as a result of preferential tax treatments to specific sectors, activities, regions, or economic agents.

References

Alesina, A., and S. Ardagna, 2009, "Large Changes in Fiscal Policy: Taxes versus Spending," NBER Working Paper No. 15439 (Cambridge, Massachusetts: National Bureau of Economic Research).

Alesina, A., and R. Perotti, 1995, "Fiscal Expansions and Adjustments in OECD Countries," *Economic Policy,* Vol. 10, No. 21, pp. 207–49.

Allard, C., and L. Everaert, 2010, "Lifting Euro Area Growth: Priorities for Structural Reforms and Governance," IMF Staff Position Note 2010/19 (Washington: International Monetary Fund).

Baldacci, E., N. Belhocine, G. Dobrescu, S. Mazraani, and I. Petrova, 2011, "Assessing Fiscal Stress," IMF Working Paper (forthcoming; Washington: International Monetary Fund).

Baldacci, E., and M.S. Kumar, 2010, "Fiscal Deficits, Public Debt, and Sovereign Bond Yields," IMF Working Paper 10/184 (Washington: International Monetary Fund).

Beetsma, R., G. Massimo, and P. Wierts, 2009, "Planning to Cheat: EU Fiscal Policy in Real Time," *Economic Policy*, Vol. 24, No. 60, pp. 753–804.

Bornhorst, F., N. Budina, G. Callegari, A. El Ganainy, R. Gomez Sirera, A. Lemgruber, A. Schaechter, and J. Beom Shin, 2010, "A Status Update on Exit Strategies," IMF Working Paper 10/272 (Washington: International Monetary Fund).

Brereton, L., and V. Vasoodaven, 2010, "The Impact of the NHS Market: An Overview of the Literature" (London: CIVITAS—Institute for the Study of Civil Society).

Cheasty, A., E. Baldacci, J. McHugh, I. Petrova, and A. Senhadji, 2011, "Indicators of Fiscal Vulnerability and Fiscal Stress," IMF Working Paper (forthcoming; Washington: International Monetary Fund).

Committee for a Responsible Federal Budget, 2010, "Principle #5: Continued Vigilance in Health Reform" (Washington).

Cottarelli, C., 2011, "The Risk Octagon: A Comprehensive Framework for Assessing Sovereign Risks," presentation at the Sapienza University in Rome on January 25 and at Politeia in London on January 26. Available via the Internet: http://www.imf.org/external/np/fad/news/2011/docs/Cottarelli1.pdf

Crawford, I., M. Keen, and S. Smith, 2010, "VAT and Excises," in *Dimensions of Tax Design: The Mirrlees Review,* ed. by J. Mirrlees, S. Adam, T. Besley, R. Blundell, S. Bond, R. Chote, M. Gammie, P. Johnson, G. Myles, and J. Poterba (Oxford: Oxford University Press for Institute for Fiscal Studies).

Cutler, D., 2004, *Your Money or Your Life: Strong Medicine for America's Healthcare System* (New York: Oxford University Press).

Dattels, P., R. McCaughrin, K. Miyajima, and J. Puig, 2010, "Can You Map Global Financial Stability?" IMF Working Paper 10/145 (Washington: International Monetary Fund).

Easterly, W., 1999, "When Is Fiscal Adjustment an Illusion?" *Economic Policy,* Vol. 14, No. 28, pp. 55–86.

Escolano, J., A. Shabunina, and J. Woo, 2011, "The Puzzle of Persistently Negative Interest Rate–Growth Differentials," IMF Working Paper (forthcoming; Washington: International Monetary Fund).

European Commission, 2009, "Aging Report: Economic and Budgetary Projections for the EU-27 Member States (2008–60)," European Economy 2/2009 (Luxembourg: Office for Official Publications of the European Communities).

Giavazzi, F., T. Jappelli, and M. Pagano, 2000, "Searching for Non-Linear Effects of Fiscal Policy: Evidence from Industrial and Developing Countries," *European Economic Review*, Vol. 44, pp. 1259–89.

Glaeser, E.L., and J.M. Shapiro, 2002, "The Benefits of the Home Mortgage Interest Deduction," NBER Working Paper No. 9284 (Cambridge, Massachusetts: National Bureau of Economic Research).

Hillestad, R., J. Bigelow, A. Bower, F. Girosi, R. Meili, R. Scoville, and R. Taylor, 2005, "Can Electronic Medical Record Systems Transform Healthcare? An Assessment of Potential Health Benefits, Savings, and Costs," *Health Affairs*, Vol. 24, No. 5, pp. 1103–19.

Iara, A., and G.B. Wolff, 2010, "Rules and Risk in the Euro Area: Does Rules-Based National Fiscal Governance Contain Sovereign Bond Spreads?" *European Economy Economic Papers* 433, December (Brussels).

International Monetary Fund (IMF), 2008, "Fuel and Food Price Subsidies— Issues and Reform Options," IMF Policy Paper (Washington: International Monetary Fund). Available via the Internet: www.imf.org/external/np/pp/eng/2008/090808a.pdf

———, 2010a, "Macro-Fiscal Implications of Health Care Reforms in Advanced and Emerging Economies," IMF Policy Paper (Washington: International Monetary Fund). Available via the Internet: www.imf.org/external/np/pp/eng/2010/122810.pdf

———, 2010b, *Fiscal Monitor—Navigating the Fiscal Challenges Ahead*, May (Washington: International Monetary Fund).

_____, 2010c, "Emerging from the Global Crisis: Macroeconomic Challenges Facing Low-Income Countries," IMF Policy Paper (Washington: International Monetary Fund). Available via the Internet: www.imf.org/external/np/pp/eng/2010/100510.pdf

_____, 2010d, *Fiscal Monitor—Fiscal Exit: From Strategy to Implementation*, November (Washington: International Monetary Fund).

_____, 2010e, "From Stimulus to Consolidation: Revenue and Expenditure Policies in Advanced and Emerging Economies," IMF Staff Paper 10/64 (Washington: International Monetary Fund).

_____, 2010f, "Fiscal Rules—Anchoring Expectations for Sustainable Public Finances," IMF Staff Paper (Washington: International Monetary Fund). Available via the Internet: www.imf.org/external/np/pp/eng/2009/121609.pdf

_____, 2011a, *World Economic Outlook*, April (Washington: International Monetary Fund).

_____, 2011b, *Global Financial Stability Report*, April (Washington: International Monetary Fund).

_____, 2011c, *Regional Economic Outlook: Europe*, May (Washington, International Monetary Fund).

Irwin, T., 2011, "Fiscal Tricks and Fiscal Transparency," IMF Working Paper (forthcoming; Washington: International Monetary Fund).

Jaramillo, L., 2011, "Public Debt, Sovereign Credit Ratings, and Bond Yields in Advanced Economies," IMF Working Paper (forthcoming; Washington: International Monetary Fund).

Jaramillo, L., and C.M. Tejada, 2011, "Sovereign Credit Ratings and Spreads in Emerging Markets: Does Investment Grade Matter?" IMF Working Paper No. 11/44 (Washington: International Monetary Fund).

Joumard, I., C. Andre, and C. Nicq, 2010, "Health Care Systems: Efficiency and Institutions," Economics Department Working Paper No. 769 (Paris: Organization for Economic Cooperation and Development).

Koen, V., and P. van den Noord, 2005, "Fiscal Gimmickry in Europe: One-Off Measures and Creative Accounting," OECD Economics Department Working Paper No. 417 (Paris: Organization for Economic Cooperation and Development).

Laeven, L., and F. Valencia, 2010, "Resolution of Banking Crises: The Good, the Bad, and the Ugly," IMF Working Paper No. 10/146 (Washington: International Monetary Fund).

Mauro, P., ed., 2011, *Chipping Away at the Public Debt: Sources of Failure and Keys to Success in Fiscal Adjustment* (Wiley, forthcoming).

Or, Z., and U. Hakkinen, 2010, "DRGs and Quality: For Better or Worse," paper prepared for the Eighth European Conference on Health Economics, Helsinki, July 7–10. Available via the Internet: http://eurodrg.projects.tu-berlin.de/publications/DRGs%20and%20quality-Helsinki.pdf

Organization for Economic Cooperation and Development (OECD), 2004, *Best Practices Guidelines—Off Budget and Tax Expenditures* (Paris).

———, 2010a, *Tax Expenditures in OECD Countries* (Paris).

———, 2010b, "Choosing a Broad Base–Low Rate Approach to Taxation," Tax Policy Study No. 19 (Paris).

———, 2010c, *Financial Market Trends*, Vol. 2009, Issue 2 (Paris).

———, 2010d, *Central Government Debt: Statistical Yearbook 2000–09* (Paris).

Saez, E., 2004, "The Optimal Treatment of Tax Expenditures," *Journal of Public Economics*, Vol. 88, pp. 2657–84.

Tokman R., M. Rodriguez, and C. Marshall, 2006, "Las excepciones tributarias como herramienta de política pública," *Estudios Públicos*, No. 102, pp. 69–112.

United Kingdom, Debt Management Office, 2010, *Quarterly Review*, October–December 2010 (London).

United States, Congressional Budget Office (CBO), 2008, *Evidence on the Costs and Benefits of Health Information Technology*, Publication No. 2976 (Washington: U.S. Government Printing Office).

United States, Department of Treasury, Financial Management Service, various years, *Financial Report of the United States Government* (Washington). Available via the Internet: http://www.fms.treas.gov/fr/index.html.

United States, Department of Treasury, Office of Debt Management, 2011, presentation to the Treasury Borrowing Advisory Committee, February 1 (Washington).

United States, National Commission on Fiscal Responsibility and Reform, 2010, "The Moment of Truth" (Washington). Available via the Internet: http://www.fiscalcommission.gov

United States Senate, Joint Committee on Taxation, 2008, *Tax Expenditures for Health Care: Hearing Before the Senate Committee on Finance*, July 30, 2008 (JCX-66-08) (Washington: Government Printing Office).

Villela, L., A. Lemgruber, and M. Jorrat, 2010, "Tax Expenditure Budgets," IDB Working Paper No. 179 (Washington: Inter-American Development Bank).